The Marketing Plan

The
Marketing
Plan

How to Prepare and Implement It

4TH EDITION

William M. Luther

AMACOM
American Management Association
New York • Atlanta • Brussels • Chicago • Mexico City • San Francisco
Shanghai • Tokyo • Toronto • Washington, D.C.

Bulk discounts available. For details visit:
www.amacombooks.org/go/specialsales
Or contact special sales:
Phone: 800-250-5308
E-mail: specialsls@amanet.org
View all the AMACOM titles at: www.amacombooks.org

This publication is designed to provide accurate and authoritative infor-mation in regard to the subject matter covered. It is sold with the under-standing that the publisher is not engaged in rendering legal, accounting, or other professional service. If legal advice or other expert assistance is required, the services of a competent professional person should be sought.

Library of Congress Cataloging-in-Publication Data

Library of Congress Cataloging-in-Publication Data

Luther, William M.
* The marketing plan : how to prepare and implement it /*
*   William M. Luther.—4th ed.*
*   p.   cm.*
*   Includes bibliographical references and index.*
*   ISBN-13: 978-0-8144-1693-8*
*   ISBN-10: 0-8144-1693-4*
*   1. Marketing.   I. Title.*
* HF5415.L83 2011*
* 658.8'02—dc22*

                    2010039115

3 9547 00360 6915

Printing number
10   9   8   7   6   5   4   3   2   1

Complete your written marketing plan by the end of the book!

The Marketing Plan

4th Edition

How to Prepare and Implement It
with "what if" software on the AMACOM website
(www.amacombooks.org/go/MarketingPlan4).

To my wonderful wife,
Betty

Contents

**Marketing Plan "what if" software models
are available free of charge at:
www.amacombooks.org/go/MarketingPlan4**

Acknowledgments

This book has been improved immeasurably by the developmental guidance of my wonderful editor, Ellen Kadin, who helped me take the manuscript from a rough twenty-page proposal and some software to this completed tome. Along the way, the manuscript had valuable input from William Helms III, Ellen's editorial assistant and right-hand man, and Debbie Posner, the copyeditor-slash-martinet who wrestled with all the particulars. This is a better book because of all of their efforts. Thank you.

Thanks also to the associate editor, Mike Sivilli, and all the hard-working people who got this book to the printer on time.

Introduction

The fourth edition of *The Marketing Plan* differs in a number of ways from its predecessor, published ten years ago. It includes ten more years of the experiences and knowledge gained from helping companies write their marketing plans—in boom economies and in bust. The book walks you through every part of the plan, with detailed analysis of case histories. After reviewing each case, you can insert on the accompanying software the data for your own company and complete your marketing objectives and strategies. By the time you finish the book, you can have a complete, written marketing plan for your own business.

If you go to the AMACOM website, you can download my computer marketing plan "what if" software models, free of charge. These allow you to insert your *own* data into the files and see the results for your business. The web address is www .amacombooks.org/go/MarketingPlan4. For best results and ease of use, you should download the software to either a CD or your hard drive. Then you can go try different data until you get the results you are seeking, such as the most effective positioning of your business, your best target audience, most favorable pricing, sufficient advertising and sales promotion weight, viable public relations plans, and enviable customer service plans. This edition can also better help you develop a popular Internet site and enable you to become a strong player in the new world of social media.

The software comes in three parts: case history "what if" files; "what if" files with formulas for inserting your own company data; and marketing plan (and other) worksheets where you insert your objectives and strategies. Although the book discusses each case history, at your leisure you should bring up these files and alter some of the inserted data and then look at the resulting outcomes. Practicing on the case history files will enable you to see how the formulas work before you start inserting your company data into your own section of the software.

The software is easy to use. You use a spreadsheet like Microsoft Excel for the "what if" files and a word processing program like Microsoft Word for the marketing plan objectives and strategies and other worksheets. The files that have a "C" in front of the name are the case histories. The file names that do not begin with a "C" before the name are the modules into which you insert your own company data.

When these files are completed, you should print them out and put them into a document called a "fact book." This is supporting data for your objectives and strategies and by inserting the files in this different document, you keep your actual marketing plan short and concise—so everyone will read and act on it. Your fact book will probably number over a hundred pages and your marketing plan should only consist of your objectives and strategies and therefore can be less than twenty pages. The third part of the software, in the folder labeled "Worksheets," contains Word files into which you can insert your objectives and strategies for each component of your marketing plan, along with other useful worksheets. If you complete each module as you go through the book, your plan will be written by the end of the last chapter.

The marketing plan belongs on the top of the desk of everyone involved with marketing so it can constantly be monitored; the fact book can go on their shelves. If you began to miss an objective, you return to the fact book and make the necessary changes to support your *revised* objectives and strategies.

Before showing a list of all the files in the software you will download, let's examine the components of a marketing plan as illustrated in Figure Introduction-1. Each of these plans is discussed in the book.

Figure Introduction-1   Components of a marketing plan.

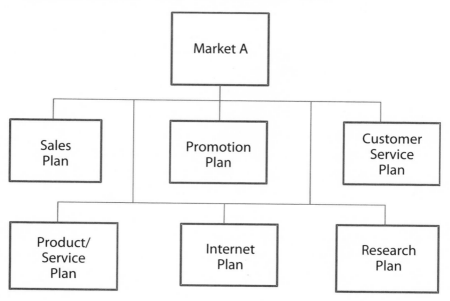

Below is a list of the computer files as they pertain to the components above and the chapter in which they are discussed.

Chapter 1	The Planning Process	No files
Chapter 2	Marketing Management	No files
Chapter 3	Market Analysis	Worksheet (your data)
Chapter 4	Customer Analysis	CCUST (case history)
		CUST (your data)
Chapter 5	Brand Development	No files
Chapter 6	The Product/Service Plan	CEXCURVE (case history)
		EXCURVE (your data)
		Objectives and Strategies (your data)
Chapter 7	Calculating Your Marketing Communications Budget	Worksheets (your data)
Chapter 8	Competitive Analysis	Worksheets (your data)
Chapter 9	The Advertising Plan	CRF (case history)
		RF (your data)
		Creative Strategy (your data)
		Objectives and Strategies (your data)
Chapter 10	The Sales Promotion Plan	CTRADE (case history)
		TRADE (your data)
		Objectives and Strategies (your data)
Chapter 11	The Public Relations Plan	Objectives and Strategies (your data)
Chapter 12	The Sales Plan: Pricing	CPRICE (case history)
		PRICE (your data)
Chapter 13	The Sales Plan: Future Sales	CSALES (case history)
		SALES (your data)
		Objectives and Strategies (your data)
Chapter 14	The Customer Service Plan	Objectives and Strategies (your data)
Chapter 15	Maximizing High-Potential Accounts	Worksheets (your data)
Chapter 16	The Internet Plan	Objectives and Strategies (your data)
Chapter 17	The Research Plan	Objectives and Strategies (your data)
Chapter 18	Pulling the Plan Together	Overall Objectives and Strategies (your data)

In the customer analysis section, you determine which market segment is best, who is involved in the buying decision, what is their ranking in importance, and what benefits each are seeking from products or services in your industry. You then do a report card on your product or service versus the competition on your ability to deliver these benefits.

In the product/service plan section, you determine the positioning of your business by using the experience curve to test the various possibilities and the resulting effects on your company. Choices include lower pricing (the Wal-Mart model), value added (Cisco), heavy promotional weight (Procter & Gamble), advanced sales techniques (IBM), effective customer service (Disney), and superior manufacturing (Apple). Apple also excels in marketing, the most recent example being Steve Jobs's decision to provide free cases for Apple's new iPhone 4 to correct the malfunctioning antenna.

In the advertising plan section, you determine the advertising weight you need by using reach and frequency analysis. Reach is the number of potential customers who have the opportunity to see and hear your message, and frequency is the number of times they have that opportunity during a particular time period. In the sales promotion plan, you analyze various activities by comparing their respective costs against the value of a sales presentation and resulting profit. In the public relations plan section, you determine which activities will give you the greatest amount of free publicity.

In the pricing section of the sales plan, you learn that you should not price to obtain the maximum amount of sales or the greatest marginal income per unit, but rather, the greatest total amount of marginal income. In the second chapter on the sales plan (future sales), you calculate all the factors that determine a sale and profit—including customer awareness, distribution, trial, repeat sales, units per purchase, price per purchase, costs, profit, and market share.

In the customer service plan section, you determine how to change this part of your business from being a department into an attitude that permeates every aspect of the business, not just the customer service desk.

In the Internet plan section, you are shown sources that will help you develop the type of website you should have, improve your keywords, and get listed on the search engines, as well as enable you to take advantage of all the opportunities available on social media. In the research plan section, benchmark studies, focus groups, and other types of research are discussed, showing you how to keep monitoring your marketing plan.

Each of the "what if" files have several ranges and after you load a file, their names will appear on the drop-down menu on the left-hand side of the screen under the word "clipboard," as shown in Figure Introduction-2. If they do not appear at first, click on the little down arrow about a third of the way down on the left-hand column. When you click on one of the ranges, the computer will take you to that part of the file. Note also that many of the files also have some charts; these are listed along the bottom of the spreadsheet, and need only be clicked on to appear. The ranges for each of the files are reproduced inside the appropriate chapter in the book. As you go through the book, you should open the files referred to in each chapter. For example, in Chapter 4, Customer Analysis, the files discussed are CCUST.xls for the case history and CUST.xls for your data.

As you go through the book, fill out the worksheets that accompany the chapters, as they are an integral part of—in fact, they comprise—your final marketing plan.

Figure Introduction-2   Examples of range names within a file.

1 · The Planning Process

Someone (I'd love to give proper credit, but don't know to whom) described the anatomy of a business shown in Figure 1–1 below:

Figure 1–1 Anatomy of a business.

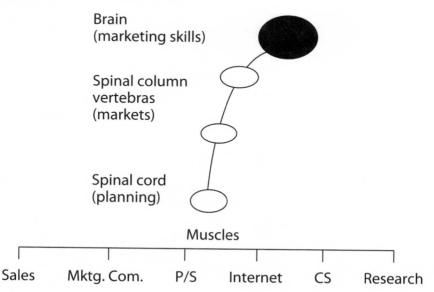

Brain
(marketing skills)

Spinal column
vertebras
(markets)

Spinal cord
(planning)

Muscles

Sales   Mktg. Com.   P/S   Internet   CS   Research

I'm hoping this book will add a few things upstairs and strength your muscles.

A Strategic Plan Is Your First Order of Business

Any planning for a business should start with a strategic plan. A strategic plan is a long-range plan, but not all long-range plans are strategic. In strategic planning you start with an analysis of the markets relative to what you are doing now and you attempt to determine what you could be doing in the future for maximum profitability.

First, of course, you must determine your market. A market is a group of potential or current customers that have a similar need or desire—or what you believe they will want or need—and share a common group of competitors, distribution channels, and packaging.

You need only look out the window to see the markets passing by. If Microsoft had been looking out the window, it would have entered the search engine business years ago, long before Google got so strong. Microsoft made a failed attempt to purchase Yahoo! and is attempting to play catch-up by introducing its own search engine, Bing. Not there yet: its recent market share (summer 2010) of all U.S. search engines, according to comScore, was only 13.6 percent versus Yahoo at 20.1 percent and Google at 61.6 percent.

Conversely, Cisco, the worldwide leader in networking, has made four major acquisitions in 2009, including Norway's Tandberg, which is in the video conferencing market.

You should not confuse strategic planning with Six Sigma. Six Sigma is a business management strategy that can help you improve your bottom line. It seeks to improve the quality of process outputs by identifying and removing the causes of defects and variability in manufacturing and business processes.

That's great, but Six Sigma should only be used after you decide which way you are headed in the future. Your strategic planning process should lead you to determine where you can make good money by increasing the value or cutting price in a current or future strength area in which the competition is least apt to follow.

My interpretation of the phrase "looking out the window" is shown in Figure 1–2 below.

Figure 1–2   Innovation.

There are three "windows" you should be looking out of. The first involves the present customer groups and I recommend that it account for about half of your efforts. The second involves adjacent markets, from which you hope to acquire new customer groups. That is, you are innovating in a business area adjacent to your core business. This should account for about 30 percent of your efforts. The third thing you should be looking for is entirely new markets, where you are expanding outside of your core business. I recommend that this activity account for about 20 percent of your resources.

Examples of the second strategy are MillerCoors LLC testing the sale of $20.00 draft beer systems for consumers to drink at home, PepsiCo purchasing independent soft drink bottlers, and Oracle purchasing Sun Microsystems. Examples of the third strategy are DuPont going from textiles to science-based industries and the *San Francisco Examiner* going on YouTube.

Unlike many other consultants, I believe that the strategic

plan should not be developed by just the board of directors and top management, but that managers and line personnel should also be included. For example, when you analyze markets, you should determine what the customers want, what are the benefits that turn them on—and no one can do that better than your marketing team. That is why the marketing plan, as well as other business component plans, should be developed alongside of the strategic plan.

According to Ted Mininni, president of Design Force, Inc.:

For brands to be truly resonant, new thinking must permeate the entire company from top to bottom. Today's successful brands must:

- Be disruptive and creative. OXO has redesigned the most mundane of objects like the measuring cup and vegetable peeler in a whole new way to make it easier for everyone, especially aging and handicapped people, to easily execute household chores, creating strong brand adherents.
- Generate excitement. The master at this, Apple, built buzz around the imminent launch of its new, long-awaited iPad . . . ambitiously stating the company is going to carve out a new product category—yet again!
- Entertain. Unilever's Axe brand of grooming products ingeniously aims at a young men's market by focusing on building a brand that ensures positive experiences between them and young females in a modern version of the Dating Game.
- Engage. Crayola continues to engage even today's high-tech kids. By moving away from its former branding as an art supply company to a provider of childhood creativity, the brand remains vibrant and relevant.

- Add convenience to consumers' lives. Staples Easy button infers home offices and businesses will easily find the products they need; enjoy expert service, advice, and substantive help like computer repair service. Simple, direct, effective branding. . . .

But here's an important point: brands can't simply launch one exciting concept and then sit back. They have to continue to create excitement. If that sounds tough—not every company can be like Apple right?—it may not be as hard as it sounds. Creativity and innovation feeds on itself and brands can borrow a page from companies that are far smaller than Apple or Google.[1]

For more information on how to develop your strategic plan, go to my website (www.wml-marketing.com) and examine the software I have for sale.

Beyond the Strategic Plan

After the strategic plan comes the business plan. The strategic plan should project the company five to ten years into the future and the business plan executes the strategic plan in more detail for the first two or three years. The business plan encompasses the entire business and includes information about the various components of the business, including marketing.

The third level of plans are the individual plans for the various components, such as the marketing, sales, and pricing plans, that are the greatest in detail and usually have a time period of one year.

In examining your markets, you want to determine what benefits your product/service can or will offer to the customer. Figure 1–3 shows an ad for a law firm in New York with the

Figure 1–3   Law firm.

Flemming Zulack Williamson Zauderer LLP

THE GO-TO LAW FIRMS® OF THE WORLD'S LEADING COMPANIES

COMPLEX BUSINESS LITIGATION

I n these difficult economic times, when so much is at stake for the business community, choosing the right law firm is critical. For almost four decades, *Fortune* 500 companies and smaller businesses alike have turned to litigation boutique Flemming Zulack Williamson Zauderer LLP (FZWZ) to represent them in the kind of complex commercial disputes that often threaten their very survival. These clients have become FZWZ clients for life.

Standing: Gerald G. Paul; Mark C. Zauderer; Linda M. Marino; Richard A. Williamson; Lissa C. Gipson
Seated: Jonathan D. Lupkin; Cathi A. Hession; Dean R. Nicyper

The loyalty of FZWZ's clients, and their willingness to entrust FZWZ with matters so important to their businesses, is easy to explain. With its approximately 35 attorneys—all of whom come to FZWZ after attending the nation's top law schools and/or practicing in the country's leading law firms—FZWZ is able to provide its clients with the high quality legal representation that is expected from a large law firm, but with the personalized attention and greater efficiency of a small firm.

Richard A. Williamson, who is featured on the cover of this year's issue and is pictured here along with some of the firm's other partners, has been an FZWZ partner since 1977. Mr. Williamson exemplifies the sophisticated and diversified nature of FZWZ's business litigation practice. Over the past 30 years, Mr. Williamson has represented clients in a wide array of commercial litigations, trials, and appeals. As just a sampling, Mr. Williamson and the firm recently have been retained to represent clients in disputes relating to Bernard Madoff's massive Ponzi scheme, the Reserve Primary Fund's "breaking the buck," auction rate securities, General Motors' revolving credit

line, and other cutting-edge business litigations. Mr. Williamson is also representing one group of clients in prosecuting the largest property damage claims in history.

Mr. Williamson has earned the respect of his clients, his adversaries, and the judges before whom he regularly appears because of his keen intellect, his seemingly endless supply of energy, his unparalleled dedication, and his ability to shepherd even the most complicated matters through the judicial process, almost invariably toward a favorable outcome. At a time when selecting a lawyer is more important than ever, clients can rest assured that Mr. Williamson and FZWZ are well-equipped to tackle their most significant business litigation matters.

FLEMMING ZULACK WILLIAMSON ZAUDERER LLP

One Liberty Plaza
New York, NY 10006-1404
Tel: 212.412.9500 Fax: 212.964.9200
www.fzwz.com

headline, "Flemming Zulack Williamson Zauderer LLP." Now, if the market is individuals looking for a law firm to hire, would that headline turn them on?

I don't think so.

Figure 1–4   Mandarin Oriental, The Hotel Group.

Figure 1–4 shows an ad for Mandarin Oriental, The Hotel Group. It doesn't really have a headline unless you are referring to the words, "He's a fan." In the small type below the picture it tells you that the name of the person sitting in the chair

is Dennis Hopper and provides a URL "to find out why [he's] a fan . . ."

Even if the celebrity shown were Roger Federer and Rafa Nadal rolled into one, would this endorsement provide those looking for a hotel a reason for staying at this one? If it doesn't find customers, it's worthless.

Now compare those two ads with the one shown in Figure 1–5 for Poise Ultra Thins. The headline reads, "When a giggle turns into a leak, turn to a more absorbent pad." If the market is incontinent women, I believe they definitely would want to know more about this product.

Figure 1–5   Poise Ultra Thins.

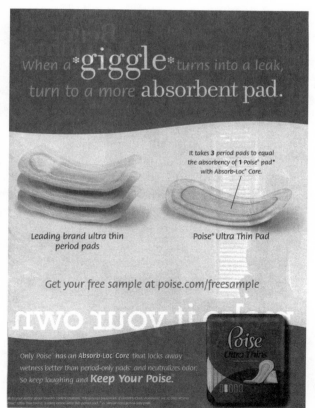

When it leaves the factory, it's lipstick; when it's opened by the customer, it's hope.

In marketing, you always want to lead with a benefit to the customer, whether it's an ad, sales call, brochure, or trade show. You then support the benefit with the features of your product/service. Fitness centers advertise that their service will build body tone and help you lose weight. That may be true, but those are features. The main reason individuals go to work out is to look more attractive. That's the benefit. Many company brochures I see have a very attractive photograph of the corporate headquarters on the cover. I could never figure out why, because they are not trying to sell their building. If, for example, you are a manufacturer of torsion bar springs for automobiles, please don't show your plant on the brochure cover. Don't even list the features of the product, such as greater storage of energy per pound. Put that on the inside of the brochure to support the benefit. On the cover you want the benefit of less weight and smaller space to increase mileage and provide more room in the automobile. You want the reader to turn the cover of the brochure, so give her a reason for going inside the brochure. Chapter 4 will be devoted to analyzing the customer.

The Fact Book, Objectives and Strategies, and Action Plans

The fact book may be the single most important "product" of your work with this book. It is the fact book that drives your marketing plan, just as the strategic plan drives which markets you should be participating in. Most of the data you insert into the various software modules we provide belong in your fact book (you have downloaded them already, haven't you?).

The objectives and strategies you write for each marketing component, based on the data you insert into the fact book, belong in your marketing plan. These are included as worksheets at the end of the appropriate chapters, and they are provided as Word files in the software package you have downloaded, in a folder called "Worksheets." As mentioned in the Introduction, the fact book may number over a hundred pages while the marketing plan should be no longer than twenty. That way you can keep your marketing plan on the top of your desk so you can monitor it weekly, with the fact book on your shelf for easy access and confirmation of your marketing plan. Many times when I was asked to review a company's marketing program, they would hand me a plan that numbered over a hundred pages. They would have a couple of meetings preparing the plan and then put it on the shelf until the following year, with no one looking at it until then. I always told them to be effective in marketing, they would have to change their planning procedure.

In addition to your fact book and marketing plan, you need action plans. Action plans provide the details of how you are going to execute your strategies and achieve your objectives. Action plans should be written and monitored by the individuals responsible for their execution. They, too, belong on the top of the desk of those executing these details.

All of your objectives should be measurable. I have been shown many plans that were just a bunch of generalities. A complete waste of time. If you can't measure your objectives, don't write them. For example, if you are using advertising, you may want to insert an awareness level you hope to achieve in your advertising plan objectives. Then you measure it and if you are off target, you should change your plan. In your sales plan, you may want to insert a closing level you hope to obtain. Once again you measure it and if you are not making it, you should make changes. You can write measurable objectives for every part of your plan. You will need research to measure some of them and Chapter 17 will show you where to find what you need.

The various components of the marketing plan will be discussed in detail in subsequent chapters. The product/service plan defines your brand. You use your advertising plan to build awareness, your direct mail plan to sell or produce leads, and your trade show plan to demonstrate what you are selling. The sales promotion plan should be used for incremental sales and the public relations plan for free ads. The Internet plan can give you instant distribution and the customer service plan can help you with repeat sales. You use the sales plan to close the sale and the research plan to monitor your activities. Appendix A contains a marketing plan format for your perusal.

Note

1. Ted Mininni, President, Design Force, Inc. of Marlton, NJ, www.designforceinc.com; www.brandchannel.com/brand_speak .asp?bs_id=231.

2 · Marketing Management

I was doing a consulting job with IBM in Canada and realized that the advertising people did not confer with the sales team and none of them talked to the sales promotion people. I ran into the same situation with AT&T. The advertising people worked by themselves and although I tried to get all members of marketing working together, it didn't work. I consequently resigned from the consulting position.

To be effective in marketing, all members of the six marketing departments must talk together and plan together. Those six departments are:

1. Sales
2. Marketing communications
3. Customer service
4. Product or service development
5. Internet
6. Research

Without working together, how can you determine which marketing tool is best against a particular member of the buying decision in a particular market? Although people are exposed to various media, you want to start with the ones they use the most. If you are going after young people, you probably will concentrate on the Internet and smartphones; for executives, maybe newspapers or business magazines; and for mom, sales promotion might work best.

In my experience, the best organizational setup is a vice president of marketing, a single individual with responsibility for and authority over *all* marketing activities, including sales. Notice that I didn't say "vice president of sales and marketing." Companies that have a vice president of sales and marketing usually treat sales as a separate entity. This leads to the situation where the sales team tells one story about the product or service and the rest of marketing tells another. That's not effective communications. Each person with common characteristics who is involved in the buying decision should receive the same message, whether it is from a newspaper ad, television commercial, website, or sales presentation. That way all messages reinforce each other. That is why you need a creative strategy, which is discussed in Chapter 9, The Advertising Plan. The creative strategy states the message and it should be used by all members of marketing.

Now, some companies that are effective in marketing, like Procter & Gamble, use the title "brand manager" rather than "vice president of marketing." The brand manager is responsible for the profit on the brand, but only has the authority on market communications, consisting of advertising, sales promotion, and public relations. That means through sheer personality and persuasion, she has to coordinate all the other marketing activities, such as sales, research, customer service, product/service plan, and the Internet. I was invited to lecture at one marketing class at Duke University graduate school of business and after talking for a while and answering questions, I mentioned that probably none of them would be hired as a brand manager at Procter & Gamble. The whole class looked puzzled and I thought the class professor was going to have a heart attack. I explained by telling them that P&G does not normally hire individuals that have a marketing degree because they want to teach them marketing themselves and they only select those that have the personality to make the system work. That is why brand management works at P&G and usually fails at other companies.

Having the Right Advertising Agency

Adverting agencies can make or break your promotional efforts. Too often, I don't remember the name of the company or brand five minutes later. Too often I don't understand an ad, and I find that too many are trying too hard to be funny, whether or not the brand lends itself to humor. What you, as a marketing manager, want is an agency that is run by a person with account management experience. That way you have a better chance of having soundness in their work. I have worked for agencies that were led by a creative person and sometimes they do good work. But let me give you an example of what can happen.

We were showing a television commercial to a client. I was an account executive and had previously told my boss that I thought it was off target. After we showed the commercial to the client, the client asked me what I thought about it. Before I could answer, my boss spoke up and said he thought it was very effective. The client than turned to me again and asked my thoughts. I said it was poor creative. The client agreed, got up, and walked out. After he left my boss told me I had just cost the agency $50,000, which was the cost of the filming, and that I was fired. We were stationed in Atlanta and the home office of the agency was in New York City. I flew up in the morning and went to see the CEO of the agency to explain the situation. Luckily he agreed with me, I was rehired and my boss was fired. The problem with this type of scenario is twofold: first, in a creative-dominated agency there is not usually someone as dumb as I to stick up for the client and second, the agency's CEO might not be as clear-sighted as this one was.

In an agency that is managed by a person with account management experience, individual account executives usually have the authority to reject creative material done by the creative department. The account executive is the prime contact with the client, is familiar with the client's business, and helps the client write the marketing plan. The creative department consists of copywriters and art directors who develop the creative upon direction from the account executive. In a creative-dominated agency, the account executive usually cannot reject creative material before it is shown to the client. That can lead to the goofy commercials that don't sell anything. Therefore, you want an advertising agency in which the account executive can reject creative before it is shown to you.

You also want an account executive who can help you write your marketing plan. When I was an account executive, the first client assigned to me was P&G. As I mentioned before, P&G has their own way of doing things and it took me five attempts before they approved of the plan I wrote. Needless to say, I learned a lot in a short period of time. A good account executive knows more about writing the plan than anyone at the company. I always wrote the plan on my accounts, including the introduction of Fresca and Canada Dry.

You also want to check out the media department of an advertising agency. Usually when individuals join an agency they are put in the media department and if they do well, are promoted to the account group or some other department.

You do not want these inexperienced people handling your media buys. If they assign you an experienced pro, then fine. If not, you should check out the media buying service companies, where the employees have been making media decisions for years.

In closing this chapter I want to repeat the hockey analogy I used in the previous edition of this book. You should buy a hockey stick for everyone involved in marketing, including your advertising agency and media buying group if you have one. The puck is your brand, the ice is the market, and the opposing team is your competition. Your objective is to get your puck into the opponent's net. You keep passing the puck back and forth, from sales, to advertising, to sales promotion, to the outside agency, to customer service, working your way down the ice. If one player gets in trouble, he passes the puck to another, back and forth, until it finally goes into the net.

Appendix B contains a comprehensive outline of your relationship with an advertising agency.

Now go buy the hockey sticks.

3 · Market Analysis

You have a wonderful idea. A better way to do something. You spend several months perfecting the concept, and then you do your launch. Sales are slow at the beginning, but after a few years, they pick up. However, you realize that you are still not making much of a profit. What's the problem? It could be one or more of several market factors that determine whether you can make money in a specific market—regardless of the superiority of your operation. There are two questions you must ask yourself at the very beginning of the process:

1. Am I going into the right market?
2. Do I have the resources to become a market leader?

This chapter concerns an important element of that "right market" question: market profit potential. If you have what you believe is a brilliant new business concept and are going to devote your life to it for several years, you want to be sure you are going into a market that will reward you well if you finish near or at the top. That reward could be money or, if you are a non-profit organization, it could be doing the most good.

Market profit potential refers to the conditions in a market that allow a business to make money if it can beat the competition. For example, a market that could be considered ideal relative to profit potential has the following characteristics:

➤ Large enough for you to obtain a good return, but not so large that you could not obtain a 30–50 percent market share.
➤ The growth rate is between 5 and 25 percent per year.
➤ The stage of life cycle is either introductory or early growth.
➤ There are few competitors and they are passive.
➤ There are no adequate functional substitutions for the product or service, and the customers perceive the item as having high value to their business or personal life.
➤ Research and development (R&D), design engineering, manufacturing, operations, and marketing costs are relatively low.
➤ The market is not capital intensive and can be segmented.
➤ The market is not seasonal or cyclical.
➤ There is no regulatory exposure.

You will probably never find a market as ideal as the above description, but the closer you come, the greater will be your opportunity to make money. To assist you in a critique of your own proposed market, each of the desirable market characteristics is discussed in this chapter to help you determine whether your venture is really worth the effort.

The following characteristics determine the profit potential in a market:

1. Market size
2. Market growth
3. Competitive strength

4. Stage of market life cycle
5. Price sensitivity
   - Functional substitution
   - Perceived value
6. Market cost structure
   - R&D costs
   - Design engineering costs
   - Manufacturing and operations costs
   - Capital intensity
   - Marketing costs
7. Market physical structure
   - Segmentation
   - Seasonality
   - Cyclicality
   - Regulatory exposure

You might want to keep a score card as you critique your market against the positive or negative effects of these factors, using Worksheet 3–1. You can photocopy it, or download it from the software and print yourself a copy. (Have you downloaded the software from www.amacombooks.org/go/ MarketingPlan4 yet and put it on your hard drive? If not, what are you waiting for?) Guidelines will be given at the end of the discussion of each factor about how you can use a scale of 1 to 10 (10 being the most favorable) to rate your market. However, any system that uses some type of pluses and minuses will suffice. At the end of this chapter you will be shown how to compile the ratings of each factor into a composite or over-all rating of the market.

This use of numbers or the assignment of values to market characteristics is not an attempt to turn planning into a science like chemistry or physics. Market planning will never be a science because the relationship between cause and effect is not

Factor	Status of Market	Value
Worksheet 3–1 Evaluating the profit potential of a market		
1. Market size	_____	_____
2. Market growth	_____	_____
3. Competition		
Number	_____	_____
Activity	_____	_____
4. Life cycle	_____	_____
5. Price sensitivity		
Functional substitution	_____	_____
Perceived value	_____	_____
6. Cost structure		
R&D	_____	
Design engineering	_____	
Manufacturing/operations	_____	
Marketing	_____	
G&A	_____	
Cost structure total	_____	_____
7. Physical structure		
Segmentation	_____	_____
Seasonality	_____	_____
Cyclicality	_____	_____
Regulatory exposure	_____	_____

Total market value (_____ **÷ 12 =)** _____

always the same in the business world. The purpose of this exercise is to make you think through each variable, one at a time so you don't miss any major ones, and to help you to estimate the effect of each on your business. Hopefully, you will judge most of them correctly, but there probably will be some you misread. This uncertainty is what makes planning difficult. It is also the reason why planning is crucial. To be successful, you have to tie down as many variables as you can and keep scrutinizing the remaining ones. Otherwise, you are going down a blind alley.

Some of you will not be able to do any scoring as you go through the chapter because you don't know the status of these factors in your market. This may mean you will have to conduct research to obtain the raw data needed in the calculations. Or you may be able to score some factors for your market, but not others. In this case, just remember to divide your final results by the number of factors you actually scored. You may also want to read the whole book before beginning this exercise, so that you are familiar with the terminology and ramifications of the various market and business characteristics.

Market Size

Normally you have to become number one or two in share of total sales or revenues in your market or segment of the market to become profitable. If you estimate that the total size of the market in which you will be competing is $1,000,000, for example, and your sales estimate is $400,000, your share objective is 40 percent. If the market is much bigger, for example, $10,000,000, your share would only be 4 percent. In this situation, unless you withdrew to a smaller segment of the market, your presence would be so small that it would be difficult to become profitable.

Usually you need a share of between 30 and 50 percent to be number one or two in your market, unless you are in a fragmented market. (A fragmented market is one consisting of many companies, all with relatively small shares, such as restaurants and barber shops. It is clearly difficult to make money in fragmented markets, and we discuss this in some detail later in the section on competitive strength.)

As a normal market shakes out, or matures, there will be a leader with approximately a 40–50 percent share. The number-two player will have a share about two-thirds of the leader or a 25–35 percent share. The number-three player will have a share about two-thirds of the number-two player or a 15–25 percent share. Experience indicates that it is tough to make significant money if you are number three or lower on the totem pole.

According to the Strategic Planning Institute (pimson line.com) in Cambridge, Massachusetts, there is a very high correlation between market share and return on investment (ROI). ROI is the rate of return on your investment. Based on the Institute's analysis of their computer database of over 2,000 businesses, in most cases the higher the share, the higher the ROI. The main reason for this correlation is the experience curve, which also is discussed in the section on competitive strength.

To score the market size characteristic, you could take your estimated share objective and multiply it by 2 and then multiply the answer by 10. For example, if your goal is 35 percent, you multiply this percent by 2, giving you 70 percent, which is .70, then multiply .70 by 10 and you get 7 on a scale of 1 to 10. That's a good score. (Or, if you don't like all this mathematics, you could score this favorable situation with a plus sign.) However, you have to be sure your share objective is obtainable. For example, if your share objective is 35 percent and you estimate the total size of the market at $2,000,000, the volume of your sales would have to be $700,000. Maybe this volume level is unattainable for you. If it is, you would have to lower your share objective, bearing in mind what was previously said about the unprofitability of being third or lower in share. This would also lower the rating of how favorable the characteristic of market size is for you.

Conversely, $700,000 in sales may be too low an estimate of

the popularity of your product or service. You could increase your share objective to 50 percent. (Going for more than half of the market is usually not profitable. You possibly could obtain a share above 50 percent, but the expenditures to get there usually can be invested more effectively in a different strategy.) A 50 percent share of $2,000,000 would give you revenues of $1,000,000—and a score of 10 (using the method above). Fantastic! However, is this enough to offset your costs? If not, you are probably going into a market that is too small. In this case, you may want to reexamine your whole concept.

Market Growth

Normally, you want to be in a growth market because it permits you to gain share even though the competition may be increasing in sales. For example, the market could be growing at the rate of 10 percent, but you are increasing your sales revenue at 15 percent. That means you are gaining share. At the same time, competition could be increasing their sales at the rate of 5 percent and be very happy, even though they are losing share. If they continue to let you gain share on them, you could eventually become so strong they could no longer compete. That was the story with American automobile manufacturers and their Japanese counterparts, although some of the American companies are now fighting their way back. It is also true with Hewlett-Packard and Dell, with Hewlett-Packard gaining share worldwide because Dell put out some defective products.

However, if you enter a market with little or no growth, the only way you can gain share is take business away from competition. Your competitors may not know when they are losing share, but they sure know when they are losing sales. This gets them very annoyed and they'll come back and try to hit you over the head. Hard. After being pounded by Wal-Mart and Target, Sears has been fighting to rebound under the leadership of its chairman, Edward Lampert, who added Kmart to the mix and made many other store changes, but success so far has been elusive. One former executive now refers to the company as a hedge fund rather than a retailer, saying that management has diverted funds from maintenance and improvement of stores to nonretail financial investments.

Many people refer to Lambert as another Warren Buffett. He says he is not interested in total retail sales, just profit. Kmart has been profitable for the last three quarters and is sitting on $3 billion in cash. He has introduced four upmarket clothing lines and beefed up the electronics department. His plan for Sears is to leave malls and build big box standalone stores. Sears' profit is tied to appliances and with housing down, sales have been weak. He did sell the $28 billion credit card line to obtain more investment income.

J.C. Penney has also been struggling with only $251 million profit in the last fiscal year, although they introduced the highly popular Ambrielle lingerie label and American Living brand by Ralph Lauren. The problem for Sears, Kmart, and J.C. Penney is Wal-Mart and Target. They lead with the discount store strategy and are now so big that it's difficult for any other retailer to compete.

If you are entering a new market, you want to maximize share as fast as your company can prudently handle the increase in sales. You want to lock out competition by lowering your costs through the use of the experience curve. Drive your costs down as fast as possible; it then becomes difficult for competition to enter.

Attaching a numerical value to market growth cannot always be linear because extremely high growth could be a negative to many companies. You may not want to be in a market experiencing a high growth rate because of the huge negative cash flow you will experience. Therefore, I suggest that you assign the "ideal market growth rate" for your company a value of 10 and score your market accordingly. In this case, growth rates both above and below the ideal would have lower scores. For example, if your ideal is a 30 percent growth, one market growing at the rate of 15 percent and another growing at the rate of 45 percent would both receive a score of 5 or some type of mark between a plus and a minus.

Competitive Strength

This is one of the most important factors that determines whether you will enjoy profitability, and surprisingly, one that many entrepreneurs don't even take into account. Actually, it's the *competition* rather than the customer that determines your revenues, market share, and profit. If you get into a market with weak or passive competitors, your opportunity is practically unlimited. You will have to scratch every inch of the way, though, if you run into an Anheuser-Busch (Budweiser, Michelob, Busch), Procter & Gamble (Charmin, Crest, Ivory), Merck (pharmaceuticals), or Cisco (computer networking).

However, don't be afraid of size alone. Witness IBM. Although one of the largest corporations in the world, it suffered tremendous setbacks in its personal computer business, which operated on such low margins that it was sold. However, in the long run it may have been smart because they are now concentrating on the high-margin consulting business.

Competitors with large market shares are the most dangerous to you when they take advantage of what is known as "the experience curve." The experience curve reflects the fact that you can cut your unit costs the same percentage rate every time you double your output. You accomplish this cost savings through the use of the learning curve, economies of scale, and throwing your weight around. The learning curve is based on the premise that as workers keep doing a task over and over again, they can do it faster and more accurately. Economies of scale are available when you increase the size or number of your plants or stores. If you built a plant twice as big as your current one, it probably won't cost twice as much to build or run. If you have to allocate your advertising over three stores, it will cost you more per store than if you could allocate the cost over twenty stores. Throwing your weight around refers to such activities as badgering your suppliers for lower costs because of the volume you buy from them and threatening the channels of distribution into handling your product or service and no others.

If a market is on an 85 percent experience curve, it means every time volume is doubled, costs will be 85 percent of what they were previously. Some industries, such as computer chips, have very steep experience curves. If a market enjoys a 50 percent experience curve rate, it means every time you double your volume, you cut your costs in half. You should estimate the experience rate that does or will exist in the market you are entering. If a competitor is much bigger than you, they have doubled their volume many times and, consequently, should have lower costs.

In Chapter 6, The Product/Service Plan, you will be shown not only how to estimate the experience curve rate for your market and competition but also how to take advantage of it to beat your competitors.

In general, a market with few competitors is usually preferred over one with many, even though it means they will have large shares. A market with few competitors, such as the oil industry, is easier to read than one with many, such as the restaurant business, which is referred to as fragmented. It is nearly impossible for any single restaurant to read the market.

Here's why: Whenever you are contemplating the execution of a strategy, you should always ask yourself, "Will competition follow?" If your answer is "I believe so," most likely the strategy will do you more harm than good. If you decide to cut your price and competition matches you, where are you? Worse off. If you double your marketing budget, and competition does the same, where are you? Worse off.

If you enter a market with just a few competitors rather than twenty or thirty, it is much easier to estimate how they will react to your strategies. In this situation, with a little homework, you could obtain a good fix on their business philosophy.

If you introduce a new product or service, will they immediately double their R&D to get into the market as soon as possible with a comparable item? Or are they relatively complacent with their current share? What will they do if you start to really make a splash? Will they still hold back? How long? Obviously, you would prefer your competition to contain a couple of Dictaphones or Sears rather than Costco and Apple.

In summary, you would like just a few competitors who are fat and happy. If you want to put a numerical rating on the competitive situation in your market, you should break it into two parts:

1. Number of competitors
2. Their anticipated aggressiveness

Regarding the number, having no competitors should rate a 10. If you have one, give it a 9, if two, give it an 8, etc. As for aggressiveness, you'll have to use your own judgment. If you believe they will match anything you do, or if they are far down the experience curve and pushing it like crazy, give it a 0. If you believe they won't pay much attention to you for a few years, give it a 5. If they look like General Motors, give it a 10. Although now they are getting better, during the past several years, GM was asleep at the switch. They did not go into small car development when gas was plentiful, and when the first gas crunch came in 1972, people switched to small cars, leaving GM out in the cold.

Stage of the Market Life Cycle

The market life cycle, which is based on the actions of your target audience, is divided into six stages:

1. Introductory or embryonic
2. Early growth
3. Late growth
4. Early maturity
5. Late maturity
6. Decline

The introductory stage refers to a brand-new market, such as 3-D television sets. Early growth refers to the early stages of a market that is really booming, like social media and iTunes. Late growth is when the market is still experiencing growth, but not quite as fast as early growth; for example, computer software and standard cell phones. Early maturity refers to the period when the market has slowed down, and all products or services are beginning to be perceived by the customer as being basically alike. Department stores are examples. Late maturity is when the market starts to shrink in size (or has shrunk), such as newspapers and CDs. Decline refers to the ending stages of the market for products such as vacuum tubes and fluorescent lights. There is no set period of time for any of the stages. The cardiopulmonary pacemaker was in the introductory stage for thirty-five years. Computer hardware had been in growth for over forty years. The hula hoop went through all six stages in one year— twice. A market can generally be in one stage while a segment of the same market is in a different stage.

Personal computers in the United States are in late growth, but personal computer work stations that permit the use of advanced software such as computer-aided design (CAD) and computer-aided manufacturing (CAM) are probably in middle growth. Market stages can also be different depending on geographical location. Soft drinks are in maturity in the United States and Western Europe, but in growth in Eastern Europe, Russia, and Asia.

Entering the market during the introductory stage—that is, your product or service is the first or one of just a few in a new market—offers you the best long-term profit potential. You have few or no competitors and you have the opportunity to become strong before others realize you have a good thing and try to muscle into your market. Companies that start new markets usually end up being the market leader. However, you have to excel in R&D and have the financial resources to hang in there until you start making a satisfactory return, which normally is not until the later part of early growth.

Some companies, like IBM, wait until early growth to enter a market. By so doing, they save on R&D costs and are in a position to copy or improve on the best technology existing in the market. It also keeps them out of markets that never make it to the growth stage. The negatives of this strategy are that they have to play catch-up and they have to excel in manufacturing and operations and marketing. In the early 1980s, Japanese companies were not strong in R&D, but they excelled in manufacturing. They would take American technology, like the electronic transistor, and adapt it to a product like radios, creating a new product. Today, not only are they preeminent in manufacturing but in R&D as well.

If you are entering in early growth, you will need the expertise to build your sales force and maximize your distribution coverage. You will want to create awareness of your product or service first, and then go for customer loyalty. You want to convince customers that they should purchase your product or service regardless of competitive activity. This is referred to as "building a franchise," and usually the best marketing tool to use is advertising. Consequently, total dollars spent on advertising by all participants in a market is the highest during the early growth stage.

If you are considering entering a market in late growth or early maturity, you can't hit competition straight on because they are too strong. (If you have developed a product or service that is clearly superior to theirs, you are not hitting them straight on; you are starting a new market.) You have to find a segment or niche in the market that competition has overlooked or that is currently too small for them to get excited about. The Japanese got their start in the automobile market by manufacturing small cars, a segment many U.S. companies were not interested in because it delivered smaller profits. The U.S. car manufacturers also correctly thought the American public wasn't interested in small cars. Then the oil shortage created higher gasoline prices, and the public demanded smaller, more economical cars. The Japanese were sitting there with the supply.

You can open a small service business such as a bank, photocopy center, or retail clothing store in markets that are in late growth or early maturity, and have the opportunity to become successful. However, you will have to offer the customer something they can't get from your bigger competitors, such as better service. The problem is the more successful you become the greater the danger of competition stepping in on your turf. If you plan on your business growing, the critical factor is whether the bigger competitors can match what you do to attract your customers. If you start selling a product such as a VCR in a market in late growth or early maturity, you have to recognize that you will be operating from a cost disadvantage. In order to make money, you will have to convince the customer that there are good reasons to pay more for your product.

Entering a market that is in late maturity or decline means that you will be operating against a shrinking customer base and you will be up against competitors that will sell their product or service with little or no profit just to stay in business. This is a market that you want to stay away from, except in some unusual circumstances. One example of an unusual circumstance is the vacuum tube business. There are only two or three companies left, and they are getting a good financial return because they bought their competitor's most efficient plants for a fraction of what they were worth and closed down their own plants, which were obsolete.

If you want to attach a numerical score to a market based on the stage of the life cycle, you could use the following:

Stage	Numerical Value
Introductory	10
Early growth	8
Late growth	6
Early maturity	4
Late maturity	2
Decline	0

Price Sensitivity

A market may be very sensitive to price increases or decreases, very insensitive, or somewhere in between. In a market that is very sensitive to price, a price increase of 10 percent would result in a decrease in volume greater than 10 percent. Conversely, a price cut of 10 percent would result in an increase in volume exceeding 10 percent. In an insensitive market, a 10 percent price cut results in a volume increase of less than 10 percent, and, conversely, a 10 percent price increase causes a volume decrease of less than 10 percent. Most entrepreneurs want a market that is relatively insensitive to price because, obviously, it offers a greater profit potential.

There are two major factors that can make a market relatively insensitive to price. One factor is that the buyer perceives the market to have products or services with no viable functional substitute. Medicine and waste management are good examples of this; there are no satisfactory substitutes for the products and services in these markets. When you are ill, you have to see a doctor. If the law states you have to dispose of your waste in a certain manner, you will do so, or get fined or go to jail. Unfortunately, this situation is not true for most markets, like restaurants, air travel, snow blowers, and artificial logs. You can eat at home or travel by car; you can shovel your own walk and cut down your own tree.

The other factor influencing price sensitivity is the perceived value of the products or services offered in the market. Logically, you don't really need alcohol, perfume, and designer jeans, but you think you do. In purchasing, perception is fact. It's not what's offered that counts; it's what you believe it offers. Therefore, if you believe exotic perfume will make you more popular, the price is secondary. How strong is the perceived value of garbage cans? You may need garbage cans more than perfume, but the customer will pay a 100 percent markup on the perfume and then shop five stores for the cheapest garbage can. To put a grade on price sensitivity in your proposed market, estimate or critique each of the two factors above, add the scores, and divide by two. Markets with no adequate substitute would receive a 10 and products/services with a high perceived value a 10 also. Where there are many substitutes, or the products/services don't have a high perceived value, the market would receive 0.

Market Cost Structure

The cost of doing business in some markets is considerably higher than in others. Many markets demand high R&D expenditures; others incur high engineering, manufacturing, or operations cost; there are those with high marketing expenditures; and several have more than one of the above negatives. The perfect market for you would be one where all of the above factors are below average in costs as a percent of sales.

A market that requires high R&D and subsequent new product or service introductions will hurt your profitability short term, and it will hurt long term if you have a low market share. One of my clients, a West Coast frozen soup manufacturer, discovered that they had been losing money for years by selling their soup to airlines. The airlines insisted on a constant stream of new types of soup. The manufacturer had never treated this group of customers as an individual market; when they pulled a separate profit and loss statement, they realized that it was an unprofitable venture.

Although having high R&D costs and needing constant innovation is a negative situation, you could build a successful company by using R&D to develop new products and services for new markets. This is the story of 3M. 3M, best known to the general public as the manufacturer of Scotch Tape and Post-it notes, introduces more new products each year for new markets than any other company in the world, and its success rate is at least equal to the best. The key to success is whether your R&D expenses will result in new revenues. If you are in a market where your new product/service just replaces an existing product or service, then R&D will account for a large percentage of costs and have a negative effect on your bottom line.

Ideally, you also want to stay away from markets with high manufacturing or operations costs. These markets usually require extensive capital investments, which means you need extremely high profits to earn a decent ROI. If your investment is $300,000, you need $60,000 in profit to earn 20 percent on your money; if your investment is only $150,000, a $60,000 profit would result in a 40 percent return.

Markets requiring large monetary investments are referred to as "capital intensive." Capital-intensive industries deliver low ROI unless the large investments produce an increase in productivity, which has positive effect on ROI.

If possible, stay away from markets that demand large investments, which, in addition to plant and equipment, could include excessive amounts of slow-paying accounts receivable and large inventory, long and expensive leases, and extensive supervisory personnel. It is true that large investments act as an entrance barrier to keep other competitors from coming in; on the other hand, they may not want to even if they could.

Although markets with high marketing costs are not considered capital intensive, markets with this characteristic can have a severe negative impact on profit potential. Marketing costs include selling, promotion, distribution, packaging, customer relations, and market research. When you combine high capital intensity and high marketing costs, you are really asking for rough sledding. If you don't obtain a major share of the market fast, you probably won't make it. Witness the airline business, which requires large investments for planes and gates and also has large advertising budgets.

Most markets for industrial products, which are usually capital intensive, typically do not require extensive marketing budgets. Therefore, if you are considering introducing an industrial product and you believe extensive marketing will be needed, it should raise a red flag. If you are considering a product or service for a consumer market, the reverse is true. Usually the marketing commitment is large, but the cost for producing the product or service is low. Some of you would probably faint if you knew the actual cost of producing some of the products you buy, like toothpaste, soap, beer, and pills for your headache and upset stomach.

Service markets normally have relatively higher costs for producing the service than consumer product markets because more labor is involved, but some enjoy high gross margins (revenues minus the cost of producing the service). Banks are a prime example of this: It doesn't cost a bank much to borrow money at 4 percent and then loan it to you at 6 percent interest. That enables them to allocate large sums to marketing. The only reason banks have gotten into trouble recently is that they became greedy and failed to realize that the value of real estate could not continually increase. In addition, they have done such a poor job of spending their marketing dollars that the number one reason for selecting a bank is still its location.

Prescription drug manufacturers have both low manufacturing and low marketing expenses, but they claim justification for their expansive operating margins (revenues minus manufacturing, marketing, and administration expense) due to their high R&D costs. A prescription that you purchase for $100 probably cost $1.00 to manufacture. However, that drug probably took ten to twenty years to develop and receive Federal Drug Administration (FDA) approval.

In summary, what you want is a market that has relatively low costs, as a percent of sales, in the four major costs centers: R&D, design engineering, manufacturing/operations, and marketing. If one cost center is above average, then, ideally, the other three should be below average. If you get yourself into a market where these costs are low, and through good management you are able to keep your own costs below the market average, your reward will be much greater than if you start off in a market where these factors leave little room to maneuver. If your market demands high marketing costs, you might develop more bang for your buck, but it will still be difficult to drastically lower the expenditure as a percent of sales.

If you want to assign a numerical score to these cost centers or factors, Figure 3–1 shows approximate ranges. General and administrative (G&A) expenses have been added so the sum equals total operating expenses, and they have been kept at an arbitrary 5 percent of sales for simplicity.

Add the percentages and calculate your estimate of your market's operating profit. If you approach 10 percent, which is

Figure 3–1   Approximate ranges of various costs as a percent of sales and resulting operating profit.

Cost Factor	Costs as a Percent of Sales		
	Favorable	Average	Negative
R&D	1–5%	5–10%	>10%
Design Engineering	1–5%	5–10%	>10%
Mfg/Operations	1–50%	50–80%	>80%
Marketing	1–20%	20–40%	>40%
G&A	5%	5%	5%
Total	<85%	85–95%	>95%
Operating Profit	>15%	5–15%	<5%

the average for the country, give this market cost structure factor a value of 5 (a plus). Any number over 15 percent deserves a 10 (a double plus). Any negative number equates to 0 (a minus). Score numbers in between accordingly. If the score is 3 or less, you should reconsider your concept.

Because the above represents an average of all markets, the ranges and assigned values are a matter of judgment and should only be used as a guide. To score your *own* market, assign percentages for each of the factors based on your critique of the market—or based on your estimate if this is a new market.

Remember, however, that this is only an *estimate* of market operating income, and does not necessary mean that you will match it. What you are looking for are markets that have the opportunity of making a good return. If you have greater resources than the competition, you probably can exceed the market average. But if you don't, or competition is more aggressive than you, your operating margin probably will be much lower.

Market Physical Structure

Four factors are included in this definition of market physical structure. They are:

1. Availability of segmentation
2. Seasonality
3. Cyclicality
4. Regulatory exposure

Two other factors that could have been described as physical characteristics are size and growth, but they were treated earlier in this chapter as separate entities.

What you are looking for are markets that have the potential for segmentation and have no seasonality, cyclicality, or regulatory exposure. In 1969 Philip Morris purchased Miller Brewing, and the strategic plan they developed for the brand called for market leadership in ten years. They almost made it. From sixth place and a 4 percent market share, they were number two with an 18 percent share eight years later and closing in on the market leader, Anheuser-Busch, which was first with a 21 percent share. Then, in 1974, August Busch III obtained control of the family business from his father, and he took the company from a 21 percent share to over 40 percent in less than ten years by successful execution of the segmentation strategy. In the early seventies, the primary brand for Anheuser-Busch was Budweiser. Today they have Budweiser Light, Michelob, Michelob Light, Busch, Budweiser Dry, and a host of other brands.

Some markets that have not been successfully segmented are gasoline, airlines, food retailing, and banking. This is because either the market does not allow segmentation or the players have been unsuccessful in executing the strategy. Gasoline, airlines, and food retailing are probably examples of the former, and banking is an example of the latter. The question for you to ask is: "Can the market be segmented successfully?" You enter the market with one product or service and obtain a 20 percent market share. You then introduce a second line. Your original line goes down to a 15 percent share, but your new line adds a 10 percent share. Now you have 25 percent share versus your original 20 percent. And so on.

A seasonal market means that some months during the year your revenues will be much lower than others. Examples are ice cream, greeting cards, skiing, flowers, and toys. If you have to carry high fixed costs throughout the year, this type of situation can be a big negative. In the skiing market of the eastern states, excellent snow conditions during the Christmas holidays and spring school break are essential; without them the best you can do for the year is break even.

If you do get involved with a seasonal market, you can flatten the revenue curve of your company by adding another business that is countercyclical, like summer activities at your ski resort. However, it has proven financially unsound to try to flatten the curve of a seasonal business. You will sell more ice cream in the winter if you increase your marketing expenditures during this time and decrease it during the high-volume summer months, but based on case histories of many seasonal businesses, you will make less money for the year. Normally, to maximize profit in a seasonal business, you want to promote the hardest during the high-volume months.

A cyclical market is one in which you enjoy a few years of high volume and then a few years of low volume. Examples are paper and forest products, metals and mining, construction, and aerospace. Once again, the critical factor in this type of market is control of fixed costs. In the paper business, when good times come, the companies expand their capacity by building new plants. When the downturn follows, they are left with excess capacity and suffer severe financial conditions. They have been doing this for the last fifty years. You would think they would learn from the past.

Like seasonality and cyclicality, you want to stay away from markets with high regulatory exposure unless you can handle these restrictive conditions effectively. Examples of markets with high regulatory exposure are pharmaceuticals, biotechnology, medical supplies, oil exploration, mining, and pollution control. You may say "Merck (pharmaceuticals) has made tons of money," and "I wish I had bought stock in Waste Management (pollution control)." It is true that these two companies are winners, but for every Merck and Waste Management, there are hundreds of companies that failed. Examples include companies that had a superior drug, a revolutionary gene technology, a machine that facilitated better medical diagnostics, a seismograph that located oil, and an environmentally protective means to discard waste. Their major problem was that they could not hold out long enough to obtain federal or state approval.

A Connecticut company offers an ultra-high-frequency jet ventilating machine for use in respiratory care that has proven advantages over existing mechanical ventilators. It took years to perfect the technology. Then empirical confirmation was obtained by using the machine on animals. After this successful step, the company now has to convince doctors in many different hospitals to use the machine on their patients. All this activity before approval by the FDA and before any revenues whatsoever. The company has already gone through many stages of refinancing, and it appears that they possibly can no longer make it on their own.

If you want to put a numerical value on your market using these four factors concerning the market physical structure, use your judgment to score each one on a scale of 0 to 10, add them up, and divide by 4. For segmentation, if your market is easy to segment, like beer, give it a 10; if it appears difficult, like airlines, it warrants a 0. For seasonality, if revenues are basically equal during the twelve months, score 10; if more than 80 percent comes within a single quarter, it deserves a 0, and if 80 percent comes within six months, score it with a 5. For cyclicality, if sales are level through the years, excluding normal growth or decline, score 10; if volume drops more than 25 percent for one or more years and then regains its previous level, post a 0. For regulatory exposure, if the market requires no governmental approval, give it a 10; if it is similar to the drug industries, give it a 0.

Total Market

I pulled together a composite chart (see Figure 3-2) of how to score the individual factors that we looked at above.

We have analyzed a hypothetical market in Figure 3-3, using the numbers from our composite in Figure 3-2, and assigned

Figure 3-2   Various conditions of market characteristics and how they affect market profit potential.

Factor	Effect on Profit Potential		
	Positive	*Neutral*	*Negative*
Market size	30–50% share	20–30% share	< 20%
Market growth	20–30%	10–20%	< 10%
Competition			
Number	0–2	3–5	>5
Activity	Passive	Average	Aggressive
Life cycle	Intro/Early growth	Late growth	Late maturity
Price sensitivity			
Functional substitution	None	Somewhat	Several
Perceived value	High	Average	Low
Cost structure			
R&D	1–5%	5–10%	> 10%
Design engineering	< 5%	5–10%	> 10%
Mfg/operations	1–50%	50–80%	> 80%
Marketing	1–20%	20–40%	> 40%
G&A	5%	5%	5%
Total	**< 85%**	**85–95%**	**> 95%**
Physical structure			
Segmentation	High	Average	Low
Seasonality	None	80% during 6 months	80% during 3 months
Cyclicality	None	Up to 15%	> 15%
Regulatory exposure	None	Few	Many

Figure 3–3   Evaluating a hypothetical market on its profit potential.

Factor	Status of Market	Value
1. Market size	25% share	5
2. Market growth	10%	3
3. Competition		
number	7	0
Activity average	5	
4. Life cycle	Late growth	6
5. Price sensitivity		
Functional substitution	Somewhat	5
Perceived value	Average	5
6. Cost structure		
R&D	1%	
Design engineering	0%	
Manufacturing/operations	45%	
Marketing	35%	
G&A	5%	
Total	**86%**	**7**
7. Physical structure		
Segmentation	High	10
Seasonality	None	10
Cyclicality	10%	5
Regulatory exposure	None	10
Total Market Value (71 divided by 12)	5.9	

values as follows: a number falling in the positive column will be given a value between 8 and 10, in the neutral between 3 and 7, and in the negative between 0 and 3.

Let's see what we have here. Figure 3–3 represents an example of a market with average profit potential. It is in late growth, growing at the rate of only 10 percent, and has seven competitors still active, but with only average aggressiveness. The products/services have only average values on functional substitution and perceived value, which is common for a market in late growth. The market operating income level of 14 percent is good, but with only a 25 percent share objective, the entrepreneur probably wouldn't enjoy this high a margin. The physical structure scores well, but with all the above negatives, the value for the market is only 5.9. Possibly, the entrepreneur should have entered the market earlier in the life cycle when there was faster growth, fewer competitors, and a greater opportunity to obtain a larger market share.

So, what is the upshot of all this work? How should you interpret the market value score of 5.9 that we generated in Figure 3–3? Should you proceed? Kill the project? The chart below is a useful tool:

Total Market Value	Comments
8 to 10	Indicates extremely high opportunity to make money if you can obtain the necessary resources.
6 to 8	Indicates a fair to good profit potential. You probably won't become a millionaire, but you should be able to pay the bills and then some.
4 to 6	Be careful. You probably shouldn't proceed unless you have unusual reasons for doing so.
0 to 4	Forget it!

Now see what you can do with the analysis you made of your own market potential using Worksheet 3–1. If you actually filled in numbers as you worked your way through the chapter, check it against Figure 3–2 and modify what needs correcting. Then add it up (again?), divide by the number of factors you were able to analyze, and see if it's a go.

If you gave up on filling it in as you went along, now might be a good time to go back and see what you can do with all this information.

4 · Customer Analysis

Many retailers no longer stock the same merchandise in all of their stores because they have realized that markets in different locations have different wants and needs. Macy's department stores recently discovered that women in Phoenix and Salt Lake City did not care for off-the-shoulder dresses. It has been said that New York has a very strong preference for black iPod models while out west consumers prefer the silver models. If you send the same sales message to the president of a firm as you do with their line personnel, most likely one or the other will not be interested; presidents are looking for different features and benefits than other members of their company. If you are treating all segments of your markets the same, you may be making a mistake.

Different market segments usually have different profit potential. I am also a commercial real estate broker and I only seek listings for raw land exceeding 30–40 acres. I believe it doesn't take any more effort or time to sell 40 acres as it does 1–5 and when I close on a sale, my income is in the high five figures.

Usually the first step in analyzing the customer is segmenting the market. You could go after just one segment that you believe offers the greatest profit potential, as I do in real estate. If you go after the entire market, then you should plan for what I call obtaining "equal share of the high potential." You should segment your market by listing the various companies or customers by their profit potential in descending order and then opposite their names insert your share of their business. If you are like several companies that have hired me as a consultant, you may have a larger share of those companies with lower profit potential. For example, your market share could be 20 percent, but you are getting 30–40 percent from the smaller potential companies and only 5–10 percent from the larger. If this is true, you should detail in your plan how you can get 20 percent from the large potential. If you achieve this goal, your profit will increase dramatically. Chapter 15, Maximizing High-Potential Accounts, discusses this concept in detail. Figure 4–1 shows the first case history from the computer software (CCUST.xls), which is one segmentation of the market. This hypothetical company sells computer software.

Final reminder to download the software from www .amacombooks.org/go/MarketingPlan4. The book is revving up, and you'll want to take advantage of what the software has to offer.

Looking at the upper-left quadrant of Figure 4–1, you will notice that the greatest profit potential for this company is consumer product companies with sales over $250,000,000; in the bottom-right quadrant, we see that new product sales accounting for 10 percent or more of total sales offers them the best profit potential. These two matrices become a description of their main target. The remaining two segmentation matrixes show that there is not a great variance in the type of consumer products or size of company. Now, as mentioned before, each of the companies in these preferred segments should be listed

Figure 4-1 Customer segmentation analysis (CCUST; range name: Segmentation).

Range Name : Segmentation

Type of Business	Estimated Potential (%)	(%)
Industrial	$100,000,000	21%
Business to Business	$75,000,000	16%
Consumer Product	$250,000,000	53%
Services	$50,000,000	11%
Total	$475,000,000	100%

Size of Company	Estimated Potential (%)	(%)
$1MM - $5MM	$20,000,000	4%
$5MM - $25MM	$30,000,000	6%
$25MM - $100MM	$50,000,000	11%
$100MM - $250MM	$75,000,000	16%
$250MM - $1,000MM	$175,000,000	37%
Over $1,000MM	$125,000,000	26%
Total	$475,000,000	100%

Type of Industry: Consumer Businesses	Estimated Potential (%)	(%)
Paper Product	$12,500,000	13%
Beer & Wine	$10,000,000	10%
Soft Drinks	$10,000,000	10%
Alcohol	$20,000,000	21%
Soap	$18,000,000	19%
Pharmaceutical	$25,000,000	26%
Total	$95,500,000	100%

New Products: % of Sales	Estimated Potential (%)	(%)
> 1%	$10,000,000	2%
1% - 2%	$15,000,000	3%
2% - 5%	$35,000,000	7%
5% - 10%	$65,000,000	14%
10% - 25%	$125,000,000	26%
Over 25%	$225,000,000	47%
Total	$475,000,000	100%

relative to profit potential in descending order and the company's market share listed opposite each one.

Now you should bring up downloaded Excel file CUST.xls, a facsimile of which is shown in Figure 4–2, and insert your own data for one or more markets. (Only insert data in the blue "active" cells; the others contain formulas and should not be touched.) You can change the headings of the various segments if you want. After you have selected the segments you should be in, then list each company or customer relative to profit potential in descending order and then opposite each company, insert your certain market share.

Yes, pretty daunting. Perhaps you want to tackle this after you have read the chapter all the way through (or perhaps after you have read the book all the way through).

After you have selected the most favorable segments, the next step is to determine the individuals involved in the buying decision. You may have a situation where there is only one buyer, but there are usually several people involved in the buying decision. A few companies I have worked with were presenting to line personnel for equipment used by line and were not making any headway. After completing some research, they discovered that as many as five other layers of the company were involved in the buying decision. Remember, when you call on a customer, he or she usually will not tell you that others can kill the sale.

Figure 4–3 presents the second part of the case history file and shows some job descriptions involved in this hypothetical purchase process.

Notice that in the Excel file we provided for you to work in, CUST.xls (see Figure 4–4), you have space to insert those who influence the purchase, those who actually make the purchase, and those who use what is purchased in *your* business. This doesn't mean you should be spending marketing dollars

Figure 4–2 Your segmentation analysis (CUST; range name: Segmentation).

Customer Segmentation Analysis

Range Name	Segmentation		

Type of Business

	Est Potential ($)	Percent
---------	$0	0%
---------	$0	0%
---------	$0	0%
---------	$0	0%
Total	$0	0%

Type of Industry

	Est Potential ($)	Percent
---------	$0	0%
---------	$0	0%
---------	$0	0%
---------	$0	0%
---------	$0	0%
---------	$0	0%
Total	$0	0%

Size of Company

	Est Potential ($)	Percent
---------	$0	0%
---------	$0	0%
---------	$0	0%
---------	$0	0%
---------	$0	0%
---------	$0	0%
Total	$0	0%

New Products - % of Sales

	Est Potential ($)	Percent
---------	$0	0%
---------	$0	0%
---------	$0	0%
---------	$0	0%
---------	$0	0%
---------	$0	0%
Total	$0	0%

Figure 4–3   Purchase process (CCUST; range name: PurchaseProcess).

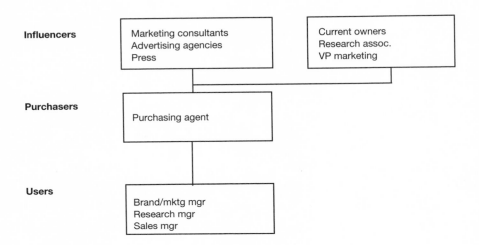

Figure 4–4   Your purchase process (CUST; range name: PurchaseProcess).

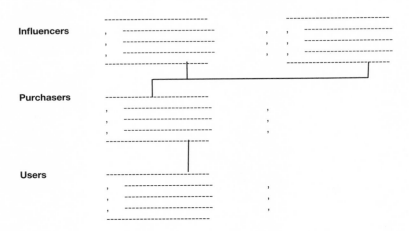

on all these individuals equally. The main reason for this exercise is so you can rank them in importance in the next step, because you want to spend your dollars against those you rank at the top.

So go to your Excel file and insert the individuals involved in your purchase process in the file shown next.

Now the next step probably requires research and examination. The task is to rank the individuals you have identified in order of importance or impact on the purchase. This can be tricky. Some cereal manufacturers thought mom came first until they realized it was the kids. Birth control manufacturers thought the doctors prescribed what they thought was best. Wrong again. It took a female marketer to tell them that women were the ones that made the decision. Likewise, many automobile dealers lost sales when dealing with female customers because they didn't think they would make a decision without their partner or husband.

Now the order in which you rank the decision makers will not be the same for all companies, but with experimentation you will see that those that are ranked at or near the top stay at the top and those at the bottom stay at the bottom. Figure 4–5, the third part of file Ccust, shows how we have ranked those whom we identified.

Figure 4–5   Purchase process priority (CCUST; range name: PurchPriority).

Range Name: PurchPriority

1. Brand/marketing manager
2. VP marketing
3. Research manager
4. Advertising agencies
5. Marketing consultants
6. Current owners
7. Sales manager
8. Research associations
9. Press
10. Purchasing agent

Notice for this hypothetical company purchasing our software there are ten individuals or job descriptions involved in the purchase process. When allocating marketing dollars for this company, you would first budget for the brand/marketing manager, then the VP of marketing, and keep going until you run out of money. As you will see later, in Chapter 9, The Advertising Plan, the messages or sales presentation should be different for each one.

Figure 4–6 shows the Excel file into which you can insert your own data. It is the third matrix presented in Cust.xls.

You want to determine what turns on each of these individuals in the purchase process. Remember, you are looking for the benefit of the product/service, not the feature (see Figure 4-7). You don't buy a Cadillac or Lexus because of its gas mileage, appearance, or drivability. You buy it because when you own one, everybody thinks you are big shot. Temple University professor Bryant Simon states that the reason Starbucks is successful is because of the lifestyle we buy with the $3 cup of joe. He continues, "Starbucks became a Wall Street favorite by making its customers feel environmentally aware, upwardly mobile, connected and

Figure 4–6   Your purchase process priority (CUST; range name: PurchPriority).

Range Name: PurchPriority

1. _____
2. _____
3. _____
4. _____
5. _____
6. _____
7. _____
8. _____
9. _____
10. _____

Figure 4–7   Benefits/features sought (CCUST; range name: BenSought).

Benefits/Features Sought Range Name: BenSought					
Benefits/Features Sought	Brand Manager	VP Mktg	Research Manager	Advertising Agency	Mktg. Consultants
Reliability: I won't make any mistakes.	5	1	1	1	2
Ease of use: Boss will think I am smart.	4	6	4	6	3
Time: I will not have to work late.	2	5	6	2	6
Cost: I'll have money left over for my pet projects.	6	2	3	5	5
Projectability: It will help me know what comes next.	1	3	2	3	1
Competitive knowledge: I love jabbing them.	3	4	5	4	4

cool by welcoming us, by name, into their clean, urban-chic stores, and pumping hip music."[1]

In this particular case, the brand manager is number one in the purchase process priority and the feature/benefit most important to her is the fact that the software allows her to project ("It will help me to know what comes next"). When talking to the VP of marketing, who is number two in the purchase process, the most significant benefit of this software will be reliability ("I won't make any mistakes"). Look at each of the cells carefully.

Now it is time for you to put in your own benefits/features in CUST.xls, and prioritize them for each of the individuals you need to influence (see Figure 4-8). First, you need to come up with various benefits for your product or service you believe the individuals in the purchase process are most interested in—and then you must rank them for each job title or customer classification.

The final step in this series is determining how well the benefits/features are delivered. Once again this will take some

Figure 4–8   Your benefits/features sought (CUST; range name BenSought).

Benefits/Features Sought   Range Name: BenSought

Features/Benefits					
-----------------	----	----	----	----	----
-----------------	----	----	----	----	----
-----------------	----	----	----	----	----
-----------------	----	----	----	----	----
-----------------	----	----	----	----	----

research, like a benchmark study (see Chapter 17, The Research Plan). The question is how well is your product/service delivering on the features/benefits desired by the people in your purchase process versus the competition. Let's take a look at our hypothetical company.

In the scoring used here, a double plus means a competitive edge, *and* that they alone deliver this feature. A single plus means the company delivers on the feature, but so do others. A zero means they do not deliver, but it is not considered a big negative, and a minus means they do not deliver and it is considered a negative.

When you look at the chart in Figure 4–9, you see five choices facing a prospective buyer to whom you are trying to sell your tracking software. "Model" stands for your new software and "STM" is a competitive product. Test marketing is of course the most reliable way to get information about a product, and will allow you to make good projections, but is difficult, time-consuming, and expensive. "No test" means "do nothing at all" (and as you can see, this is a first-class ticket on the cheap-quick-and-easy train: double pluses there). And we all know about panels (better than nothing, but . . .). These then are the options facing the individuals on how to monitor their data, and how they rate them.

Figure 4–9   Benefits/features delivered (CCUST; range name: BenDelivered)

Benefits/Features Delivered Range Name: BenDelivered					
Benefits/Features	**Model**	**Test Mktg**	**No Test**	**STM**	**Panels**
Reliability	+	++	–	+	+
Ease of use	+	–	++	0	0
Time	+	–	++	0	–
Cost	+	–	++	+	+
Projectability	0	++	–	+	0
Competitive knowledge	+	–	++	+	0

Our hypothetical company has a problem. Projectability, which is the number-one feature desired by the person at the top of the purchase process, the brand manager, only rates a zero. Reliability, sought by the number-two person in the buying decision, the VP of marketing, gets a plus, which is better than a zero, but does not give the company a competitive edge on this factor. Now take a look at your own company. Using the information that you developed for Figure 4–8, complete Figure 4–10 as best you can. You will almost surely need new research to complete the task.

Figure 4–10   Your benefits/features delivered (CUST; range name: BenDelivered).

Benefits/Features Delivered				Range Name: BenDelivered	

Note

1. Luciana Chavez, "Professor gives Starbucks a roasting," *News and Observer,* December 27, 2009; www.newsobserver.com/2009/12/27/254709/professor-gives-starbucks-a-roasting.html.

5 · Brand Development

Don't flavor your brand plain vanilla. An effective brand has a likable or admired personality. It has added perfume. Likable ones could include McDonald's, Budweiser, and Bloomingdale's. Kids love McDonald's with its premiums, especially the toys, and drag their parents with them. Bud is so likable it has the largest beer market share in the world. When women go into Bloomingdale's in New York City they go star-crazy. Admired brands could include Apple, Cisco, Intel, and Neiman Marcus. If Steve Jobs ever wore a business suit, the company that makes those sexy products would lose its luster. Cisco and Intel are "out-chipping" their competitors. And who besides Neiman Marcus would have the gall to offer $250,000 Christmas presents?

Brands that could use some help might include Sears, Toyota, AT&T Internet service, and health insurers. Sears has really gone downhill in recent years. It doesn't have a personality anymore. Toyota used to be flying high, but it now comes out that they knew of the problems with uncontrolled acceleration more than two years ago. If you want to keep your goodwill when you incur a problem, you want to tell the world as soon as possible, the way Johnson & Johnson did years ago when some bottles of Tylenol had been tampered with. I lost my Internet connection with AT&T and it took five hours and six technical support technicians to bring me back online. I need not make any comments about the health insurers.

You want to be unique, like the FedEx selling line, "When you absolutely, positively need it overnight," although it appears that they have stupidly stopped using the phrase. I had a home builder client who had twenty-five homes he wanted to sell during the next twelve months with a relatively small advertising budget. I did some research and found that most other builders usually ran full-page newspaper ads, with a few scheduling a two-page spread. I proposed a three-page spread with the front page showing a couple drinking coffee and holding up an invitation card that read, "The Homes for Elegant Living." When you turned the page, an illustration of the most attractive home was spread across the two pages, which was about twenty-two inches wide. At first the client thought I was nuts, because the ad would take up 90 percent of his entire budget. He finally agreed to let me run with it. I also had all salesmen wear white dinner jackets. The Sunday his ad ran, his subdivision was so mobbed I had to call the police to come out and handle the traffic. All of the homes were sold in ninety days—and we never had to run another ad.

You want to keep it simple. It is said that, after listening to a two-hour sermon, the First Lady asked her husband, President Coolidge, what the sermon was about. He replied, "Sin." She was a little shocked, but then asked what the pastor said about it. The president is said to have replied, in his usual taciturn manner, "He was against it." Years ago Hawaiian Punch ran a ten-second television commercial that made them number one in sales. It consisted of two cartoon characters in Hawaiian shirts, with one holding a bottle of the product. He asks the other if he would like a Hawaiian punch and when the man said yes, he leaned over and punched him in the nose.

There is a separate chapter on pricing in this book (Chapter 12, The Sales Plan: Pricing), but the main thing to remember is base your price on value, not on costs. DuPont developed a new resin for drainpipes that kept the pipe from leaking. The costs associated with using the resin were negligible, but DuPont increased the cost of the pipe 400 percent, because that was the value.

Base your development against the target audience, as discussed in Chapter 4, Customer Analysis, and don't forget the 20/80 guideline: approximately 20 percent of the market should account for 80 percent of your profitable sales. And when you have a winning personality, stay with it. Rosser Reeves, when he was president of the advertising agency Ted Bates, was on his yacht with a client who reminded Bates that he had been running the same campaign for him for the last ten years and asked Reeves how many employees he had. Reeves answered, "Two thousand." "Then," asked the client, "what are they doing for me?" Reeves's answer: "Those two thousand people are keeping your people from changing that campaign."

So, what is your brand's personality? If you are not sure, you should first obtain a statement of position, which details what your current and potential customers have to say about your company. You will probably need a benchmark research study (see Chapter 17, The Research Plan) to obtain the answers. After you complete this study, you can prepare your positioning statement.

Your positioning statement is your company's personality. It is how you want to be perceived by your target audience. It is usually written by marketing people, but it should reflect your entire operation. Everything you do should be compatible with it. Following is a positioning statement that could have been written by Bloomingdale's in New York City.

Figure 5–1   Possible positioning statement for Bloomingdale's.

Positioning Statement

1. Who: Bloomingdale's, NYC
2. What: Fashion-focused department store
3. For whom: Trend-conscious, upper-middle-class women
4. What need: Looking for high-end products
5. Competition: Other department stores
6. What's different: Unique merchandising in a theatrical setting
7. So?: It makes shopping entertaining

You may want to take a stab at writing your own now, but based on how you complete the remaining sections of this book, your initial draft may be altered. For example, in the next chapter you will determine what type of mousetrap you want your company to be and that will influence your positioning statement.

You can photocopy this worksheet or print out a copy of the positioning statement worksheet from your downloaded folder of Word worksheets.

Worksheet 5–1   Positioning statement

1. Who: _____

_____

2. What: _____

_____

3. For whom: _____

_____

4. What need: _____

_____

5. Against whom: _____

_____

6. What's different: _____

_____

7. So?: _____

_____

To execute your new or revised brand personality, you may have to increase your marketing budget and one of the best times to do so is when the economy is not doing so well. There have been many research studies that indicate that those companies that increase their marketing pressure during bad times are usually the ones that come out on top when the economy improves. And you may want to think beyond the current marketing tools you are using.

You do not have to be a large company to develop a favorable brand personality. A corporate jet refueler offers low fuel prices and fast service. It also has two women dressed in short white skirts and sleeveless T-shirts waving bright orange flags to direct pilots to its facility. But the real attraction for their customers is what's in the brown paper bag the women slip to the pilots once they pulled in to fill up—Kansas City strip steaks. Pilots say their bosses like the fuel price, but they stop there for the steaks.

6 · **The Product/Service Plan**

You have a choice of four different types of mousetraps to catch your customers. They are:

1. A better mousetrap
2. A disappearing-mouse mousetrap
3. A 36-inch mousetrap
4. A cheaper mousetrap

A better mousetrap is of higher quality than the competition. Examples are Haagen Dazs ice cream, Godiva chocolates, and Cross pens. A disappearing-mouse mousetrap is where you don't have to see the dead mouse. You can now buy mousetraps where the mouse goes into a box, like a little hotel, and can't get back out in the morning. Then you throw out the hotel. This type of mousetrap is not any more effective than the old kind, but is preferred because you don't see the dead mouse. The definition of a disappearing-mouse mousetrap is a product or service that is actually not superior to competition, but is believed to be so, due to effective marketing. Examples are Marriott Hotels, Budweiser, and British Airways.

You beer drinkers who don't like the taste of Bud and want to argue with me about classifying Budweiser as a disappearing-mouse mousetrap, you have to remember they have the largest market share of any beer.

A 36-inch mousetrap is a niche player. Examples are Hasselblad cameras, Montessori schools, and Panera Bread. A cheaper mouse trap is self-explanatory. Examples are Wal-Mart, Days Inn, and Target.

To become one of these four types of mousetraps takes money. For example, if you want to be a better mousetrap, you have to improve your business operation, either your manufacturing process, customer service, or some other aspect. At Marriott, customer service is an attitude, not a department. "Marriott is the most reliable of brands," says Bjorn Hanson, an industry analysis who now teaches at New York University's Tisch Center for Hospitality, Tourism, and Sports Management. "There is a saying in the industry that Marriott puts heads in beds."[1]

To become a disappearing-mouse mousetrap, you have to become more effective in marketing. Who doesn't love those Budweiser Clydesdales? To be a successful niche player, you have to have high quality and a large market share. Digital cameras have replaced film, but the Hasselblad is the camera that they took to the moon. Mention Panera Bread and fans are as likely to praise the free Wi-Fi as they are to gush about the Asiago cheese bagels. And that, execs at the $2.6 billion restaurant chain say, is the point. While its competitors scale back on upscale ingredients, trim portion sizes, and create value menus, Panera is selling fresh food and warm bread at full price and encouraging customers to linger. That recipe is succeeding.[2]

Responding to competition, Starbucks is now starting to offer free Wi-Fi in their stores.

To be a cheaper mousetrap, you have to increase your productivity so you will be the best in operational efficiency. Wal-Mart has more screens at their home base than the three television networks combined. They show every step of their distribution process around the world.

Because more expenditures are needed to execute any of these strategies, a good system to use is the experience curve to determine whether the costs are justifiable. The experience curve concept was initially labeled the learning curve. During World War II, an Air Force general recognized that as we kept assembling more and more B-17 bombers, the workforce was able to assemble each one in less time. As labor spent more time on the job, they became more adept at what they were doing, adapted better processes, became more specialized, and so on. The result was increased productivity. This concept is considered just common sense today, but back then it was revolutionary.

In subsequent years, management realized that savings due to increased productivity were possible from many areas besides labor. There were economies of scale. If a 10-million-ton oil refinery cost $10 million to build and took 5,000 employees to operate, a 20-million-ton refinery does not cost $20 million to build and take 10,000 employees to operate. Rather, approximately $15 million and 7,500 employees. As companies bought larger amounts from their suppliers, they could demand lower prices and better terms. Marketing costs could also be lowered. It doesn't cost ten times as much to advertise ten stores in a city as it does for one.

The sum of all these savings is referred to as "the experience curve" and the concept is that in industries where these savings are applicable and you take advantage of them, your costs will decrease approximately the same percent each time you double your volume. If your costs in real dollars after you double your volume are 85 percent of previous figures, then you are on an 85 percent experience curve. Notice that it's based on doubling of volume, not on time. Therefore, you can use the experience curve to check the feasibility of adapting one of the above strategies.

Calculating the Experience Curve

To begin, you should determine what experience curve rate you are currently on based on past costs versus today's costs. Let's look at the first case history, in CEXCURVE.xls, concerning a hypothetical company called Strategic Business Unit (SBU).

The experience curve for this company, SBU, is 89.01 percent. Their operation has three components. There is one component A per unit, two components B, and one component C, which is supplied by an outside supplier. The experience curve for component A is 84.34 percent, 87.36 percent for component B, 81.90 percent for component C, and 89.01 percent in total. (Yes, the total experience curve is calculated independently, from the total costs themselves; it is *not* an average—weighted or otherwise—of the first three curves.)

Let's examine in detail how the computer model performs. Component A costs $50 in 2002 and $30 in 2009. The experience curve concept is that costs are decreased at the same percentage rate each time cumulative volume is doubled. First-year volume (2002) for SBU X (our new product's name) was 1,000 units. There is one component A per unit so first-year volume on component A was also 1,000. First-year volume is the base on which all subsequent doubling is calculated. In 2003, volume on component A was 2,100 and the computer model recognizes that the first doubling in volume occurs (from 1,000 the first year to 2,100 cumulative by the end of the second year). The second doubling will occur when cumulative volume hits 4,000 and this happens in 2005. The third doubling will be 8,000 and this level is reached in 2008. The question to the computer model is: at what experience curve rate are costs being reduced if a component's cost is reduced from $50 to $30 during a period of three doublings? The answer is 84.34 percent, as shown in the exhibit directly under the column "# units" for component A. If you want to verify the computer model's math, multiply $50 by 84.34 percent and you will get $42.17. This should be the cost of component A after the first doubling, which occurs in 2003. Verify this cost on the exhibit. The cost after the second doubling (2005) should be $42.17 times 84.34 percent or $35.57, and the third doubling (2008), $35.57 times 84.34 percent or $30. Isn't math gratifying?

The computer model does the same calculations for component B, component C, and the sum of components A, B, and C or total cost of SBU X. For component B, two units are used for each unit of SBU X, so the first doubling occurs at 4,000 (first-year volume of 2,000 times 2) rather than the 2,000 level for component A (first-year volume of 1,000 times 2). However, even though each doubling is achieved at higher levels (first: 4,000; second: 8,000; third: 16,000; and so on) than for component A, because two units are used per unit of SBU X, component B reaches each doubling at the same time as component A.

This is not true for component C. First-year volume is 1,000 because one component is used per SBU X unit. However, the company that supplies this component to the company had produced 4,000 for use with other products before 2002. Therefore, the first-year volume is listed at 5,000 and the first doubling does not occur until 10,000 units. This level is not reached until 2006 (10,105 cumulative volume). Although the experience curve rate or cost reduction for each doubling is greater for component C (81.90 percent) than for A (84.34 percent) or B (87.36 percent), only one doubling is obtained during the period 2002 to 2009, and the cost is only reduced from $105 to $86 ($105 times 81.90

percent). The combined experience curve rate for SBU X is 89.01 percent and total cost of goods is reduced from $329 to $232 during these eight years (2002 to 2009).

This experience curve rate for the components can now be used for future costs projections. SBU can estimate that when they reach the fourth doubling (16,000), the cost for component A should be approximately $25.30 ($30 times 84.34 percent); fifth doubling, $21.34 ($25.30 times 84.34 percent); and so on.

When you use this part of the model EXCURVE.xls for your own SBUs, you may find that you have experienced no cost reductions, even after adjusting the numbers for inflation. This would probably mean that either the experience curve concept does not exist in your particular market or it does but you are not taking advantage of it. In some industries it's difficult, if not impossible, to experience savings from economies of scale, although the number of industries appears to be small. An example would be most restaurants because they tend to be labor-intensive and have high staff turnover. On the other hand, the economies could be there in your particular industry, but you have failed to realize it. Maybe you are not demanding lower costs from your suppliers due to your increased volume nor are you aggressively promoting your firm to top prospective new employees. Maybe you have not organized your company to profit from economies of scale in manufacturing, operations, advertising, distribution, sales promotion, etc.

From your books or accountant, insert your own data in the Excel file EXCURVE.xls. Only insert your data where you see the blue zeros or lines. All black zeros are formulas.

After you insert your numbers, the experience curve rate will be calculated automatically. If you have more components than shown above, just copy and paste. If you are a service company, you can change the word "component" to "service offered," "customer service," etc.

For comparison purposes, you can project yourself into the future doing what you are doing now and then compare these numbers with those of the various strategies you want to consider. The case history of our hypothetical SBU, we postulate that it is growing at the rate of 10 percent per year (see Figures 6-1 and 6-2). The projection of how this will play out in succeeding years is shown in Figure 6-3.

Now we will take a look at their complete operation, as seen in Figure 6-4. It includes the total costs, pricing, market share, and profits for our SBU.

Calculating Discounted Cash Flow

Our third and final file for the status quo shows the discounted cash flow of this plan (see Figure 6-5). Discounted cash flow is probably the single most important number that will come out of this chapter.

This is not a bad plan. If the SBU just continues doing what they have in the past, their discounted cash flow is 15 percent. Discounted cash flow is your return on your investment over time. When you complete these same three files for your company and you obtain a similar rate of return, you may not want to make any changes. Of course, if you obtain a lower rate of return, most likely you should consider changes.

I believe discounted cash flow is the most meaningful measurement of success. Profit is something made up by accountants. Try buying something at the grocery store with that figure. Besides, it doesn't take into account committed resources or time. Return on investment (ROI) adds resources to the equation, but does not consider time, and once again, it's an accounting term. However, cash flow is that green stuff in your pocket and that's what really counts. Adding time to cash flow gives you discounted cash flow or the rate of return on

(text continues on page 84)

Past Cost of Goods Experience—SBU

Range Name: **SBUpastcosts**

SBU X

2002-2009

(Units are in Hundreds)

Year	Growth Rate	# Units Prod.	Cum Vol	Component A # per unit	Component A # Units	Component A Cost	Component A Doubled	Component B # per unit	Component B # Units	Component B Cost	Component B Doubled	Component C Outside supplier # per unit	Component C Outside supplier # Units	Component C Outside supplier Cost	Component C Outside supplier Doubled	Total Cost	Total Doubled
2002		1,000	1,000	1	1,000	$50.00	0	2	2,000	$87.00	0	1	5,000	$105.00	0	$329.00	0
2003	10%	1,100	2,100		2,100	$42.17	1		4,200	$76.00	1		6,100	$105.00	0	$299.17	1
2004	10%	1,210	3,310		3,310	$42.17	1		6,620	$76.00	1		7,310	$105.00	0	$299.17	1
2005	10%	1,331	4,641		4,641	$35.57	2		9,282	$66.39	2		8,641	$105.00	0	$273.36	2
2006	10%	1,464	6,105		6,105	$35.57	2		12,210	$66.39	2		10,105	$86.00	1	$254.36	2
2007	10%	1,611	7,716		7,716	$35.57	2		15,431	$66.39	2		11,716	$86.00	1	$254.36	2
2008	10%	1,772	9,487		9,487	$30.00	3		18,974	$58.00	3		13,487	$86.00	1	$232.00	3
2009	10%	1,949	11,436		11,436	$30.00	3		22,872	$58.00	3		15,436	$86.00	1	$232.00	3
					Exp. Rate 84.34%				Exp. Rate 87.36%				Exp. Rate 81.90%			Exp. Rate 89.01%	

Figure 6-2 Your past cost of goods experience—SBU (EXCURVE, range name: SBUpastcosts).

Past Cost of Goods Experience—SBU

Range Name: SBUpastcosts

SBUX

(Units are in Hundreds)

Year	Growth Rate	# Units Prod.	Cum Vol	Component A # per unit	# Units	Cost	Doubled	Component B # per unit	# Units	Cost	Doubled	Component C Outside supplier # per unit	# Units	Cost	Doubled	Total Cost	Doubled
—	0	0	0		0	$0.00	0		0	$0.00	0		0	$0.00	0	$0.00	0
—	0	0	0		0	$0.00	0		0	$0.00	0		0	$0.00	0	$0.00	0
—	0	0	0		0	$0.00	0		0	$0.00	0		0	$0.00	0	$0.00	0
—	0	0	0		0	$0.00	0		0	$0.00	0		0	$0.00	0	$0.00	0
—	0	0	0		0	$0.00	0		0	$0.00	0		0	$0.00	0	$0.00	0
—	0	0	0		0	$0.00	0		0	$0.00	0		0	$0.00	0	$0.00	0
—	0	0	0		0	$0.00	0		0	$0.00	0		0	$0.00	0	$0.00	0
—	0	0	0		0				0				0				0
—	0																

Exp. Rate 0.00%   Exp. Rate 0.00%   Exp. Rate 0.00%   Exp. Rate 0.00%   Exp. Rate 0.00%

Figure 6-3 Estimated cost of goods experience—status quo (CEXCURVE; range name: Growthstatusquo).

Estimated Future Cost of Goods Experience—Status Quo

2010-2019

Year	Growth Rate	# Units Produced	Cum Vol	Component A Exp. Curve Units	Component A Cost (0.00%)	Component A Doubled	Component B Exp. Curve Units	Component B Cost (0.00%)	Component B Doubled	Component C (Outside supplier) Exp. Curve Units	Component C Cost (0.00%)	Component C Doubl.	Total Cost	Total Doubled
# per unit					*1*			*2*			*1*			
(baseline)			11,436	11,436			22,872			15,436				
2010	10%	2,144	13,579	13,579	$30.00	3	27,159	$58.00	3	17,579	$86.00	1	$232.00	3
2011	10%	2,358	15,937	15,937	$30.00	3	31,875	$58.00	3	19,937	$86.00	1	$232.00	3
2012	10%	2,594	18,531	18,531	$30.00	3	37,062	$58.00	3	22,531	$86.00	1	$232.00	3
2013	10%	2,853	21,384	21,384	$25.30	4	42,769	$50.67	4	25,384	$70.44	2	$197.08	4
2014	10%	3,138	24,523	24,523	$25.30	4	49,045	$50.67	4	28,523	$70.44	2	$197.08	4
2015	10%	3,452	27,975	27,975	$25.30	4	55,950	$50.67	4	31,975	$70.44	2	$197.08	4
2016	10%	3,797	31,772	31,772	$25.30	4	63,545	$50.67	4	35,772	$70.44	2	$197.08	4
2017	10%	4,177	35,950	35,950	$21.34	5	71,899	$44.26	5	39,950	$70.44	2	$180.30	5
2018	10%	4,595	40,545	40,545	$21.34	5	81,089	$44.26	5	44,545	$57.69	3	$167.56	5
2019	10%	5,054	45,599	45,599	$21.34	5	91,198	$44.26	5	49,599	$57.69	3	$167.56	5
Exp. Rate					84.34%			87.36%			81.90%			87.38%

Figure 6-4 Status quo strategy (CEXCURVE; range name: SBUstatusquo).

SBU X
Plan G

Range Name: **SBUstatusquo**

Status **Quo Strategy**
Total Costs, Pricing, Share, and Profit—SBU
(Units & Operating Income in Hundreds)

Year	Growth Rate	# Units Prod.	Cost of Goods	Sales	Prom.	CS/ Dist.	Value Added	Mfg./ Eng.	G/A	Total Costs	Sales Price	Oper. Profit	Ind. Growth	Share
2002		1,000	$329	$50	$20	$5	$0	$0	$20	$424	$400	($24,000)	10%	25%
2003	10%	1,100	$299	$50	$20	$5	$0	$0	$20	$394	$400	$6,408	10%	25%
2004	10%	1,210	$299	$50	$20	$5	$0	$0	$20	$394	$400	$7,049	10%	25%
2005	10%	1,331	$273	$50	$20	$5	$0	$0	$20	$368	$400	$42,118	10%	25%
2006	10%	1,464	$254	$50	$20	$5	$0	$0	$20	$349	$400	$74,148	10%	25%
2007	10%	1,611	$254	$50	$20	$5	$0	$0	$20	$349	$400	$81,563	10%	25%
2008	10%	1,772	$232	$50	$20	$5	$0	$0	$20	$327	$400	$129,324	10%	25%
2009	10%	1,949	$232	$50	$20	$5	$0	$0	$20	$327	$400	$142,256	10%	25%
2010	10%	2,144	$232	$50	$20	$5	$0	$0	$20	$327	$400	$156,482	10%	25%
2011	10%	2,358	$232	$50	$20	$5	$0	$0	$20	$327	$400	$172,130	10%	25%
2012	10%	2,594	$197	$50	$20	$5	$0	$0	$20	$292	$400	$279,926	10%	25%
2013	10%	2,853	$197	$50	$20	$5	$0	$0	$20	$292	$400	$307,919	10%	25%
2014	10%	3,138	$197	$50	$20	$5	$0	$0	$20	$292	$400	$338,710	10%	25%
2015	10%	3,452	$197	$50	$20	$5	$0	$0	$20	$292	$400	$372,582	10%	25%
2016	10%	3,797	$197	$50	$20	$5	$0	$0	$20	$292	$400	$409,840	10%	25%
2017	10%	4,177	$180	$50	$20	$5	$0	$0	$20	$275	$400	$520,886	10%	25%
2018	10%	4,595	$168	$50	$20	$5	$0	$0	$20	$263	$400	$631,542	10%	25%
2019	10%	5,054	$168	$50	$20	$5	$0	$0	$20	$263	$400	$694,696	10%	25%

Total Profit $4,343,579

Figure 6–5   Discounted cash flow: status quo (CEXCURVE; range name: DCFstatusquo).

Discounted Cash Flow: Status Quo

Range Name: DCFstatusquo

Year	Operating Profit	Add Back Deprec.	Initial Cost	Total Cash Flow	Discount Factor 15.00%
			$2,000,000	($2,000,000)	($34,007)
2010	$156,482	$66,667		$223,149	
2011	$172,130	$66,667		$238,797	
2012	$279,926	$66,667		$346,593	
2013	$307,919	$66,667		$374,586	
2014	$338,710	$66,667		$405,377	
2015	$372,582	$66,667		$439,249	
2016	$409,840	$66,667		$476,507	
2017	$520,886	$66,667		$587,553	
2018	$631,542	$66,667		$698,209	
2019	$694,696	$66,667		$761,363	

your resources invested over a given period of time. Calculating discounted cash flow on various plans also allows you to compare apples and oranges. If plan A is to raise apples with an initial investment of $100,000 and estimated DCF of 20 percent over five years, everything else being equal, it's better than plan B, which is to raise oranges with an initial investment of $75,000 and estimated DCF of 10 percent over the same period of time.

Figures 6-6, 6-7, and 6-8 are facsimiles of the three files we have just discussed into which you will put your data to compute *your* status quo.

Remember, only insert data where you see blue zeros. To calculate your discounted cash flow factor, keep putting percent numbers under the wording "Discount Factor" until the number below is the smallest you can obtain. For example, on Figure 6–5 the discount factor (last column on the right) is 15 percent and the number below that is 34,007. (Note that this number does not represent dollars; it is just a number, and your goal, for various arcane mathematical reasons, is to

Figure 6–6 Your estimated future cost of goods experience—status quo (EXCURVE; range name: Growthstatusquo).

Estimated Future Cost of Goods Experience—Status Quo

Range name: **Growthstatusquo**

Year	Growth Rate	# Units Produced	Cum Vol	Component A # per unit Exp. Curve Units	0.00% Cost	Doubled	Component B # per unit Exp. Curve Units	0.00% Cost	Doubled	Component C Outside supplier # per unit Exp. Curve Units	0.00% Cost	Doubled	Total Cost	Doubled
	0%	0	0	0	$0.00	0	0	$0.00	0	0	$0.00	0	$0.00	0
	0%	0	0	0	$0.00	0	0	$0.00	0	0	$0.00	0	$0.00	0
	0%	0	0	0	$0.00	0	0	$0.00	0	0	$0.00	0	$0.00	0
	0%	0	0	0	$0.00	0	0	$0.00	0	0	$0.00	0	$0.00	0
	0%	0	0	0	$0.00	0	0	$0.00	0	0	$0.00	0	$0.00	0
	0%	0	0	0	$0.00	0	0	$0.00	0	0	$0.00	0	$0.00	0
	0%	0	0	0	$0.00	0	0	$0.00	0	0	$0.00	0	$0.00	0
	0%	0	0	0	$0.00	0	0	$0.00	0	0	$0.00	0	$0.00	0
	0%	0	0	0	$0.00	0	0	$0.00	0	0	$0.00	0	$0.00	0
	0%	0	0	0	$0.00	0	0	$0.00	0	0	$0.00	0	$0.00	0
				Exp. Rate 0.00%			Exp. Rate 0.00%			Exp. Rate 0.00%			Exp. Rate 0.00%	

Figure 6–7 Your status quo strategy (EXCURVE; range name: SBUstatusquo).

Status Quo Strategy

SBU ——

Plan ——

Range Name: **SBUstatusquo**

Total Costs, Pricing, Share, and Profit—SBU

(Units & Operating Income in Hundreds)

Year	Growth Rate	# Units Prod.	Cost of Goods	Sales	Prom.	CS/Dist.	Value Added	Mfg./Eng.	G/A	Total Costs	Sales Price	Oper. Profit	Ind. Growth	Share
—	0%	0	$0	$0	$0	$0	$0	$0	$0	$0	$0	$0	$0	0%
—	0%	0	$0	$0	$0	$0	$0	$0	$0	$0	$0	$0	$0	0%
—	0%	0	$0	$0	$0	$0	$0	$0	$0	$0	$0	$0	$0	0%
—	0%	0	$0	$0	$0	$0	$0	$0	$0	$0	$0	$0	$0	0%
—	0%	0	$0	$0	$0	$0	$0	$0	$0	$0	$0	$0	$0	0%
—	0%	0	$0	$0	$0	$0	$0	$0	$0	$0	$0	$0	$0	0%
—	0%	0	$0	$0	$0	$0	$0	$0	$0	$0	$0	$0	$0	0%
—	0%	0	$0	$0	$0	$0	$0	$0	$0	$0	$0	$0	$0	0%
—	0%	0	$0	$0	$0	$0	$0	$0	$0	$0	$0	$0	$0	0%
—	0%	0	$0	$0	$0	$0	$0	$0	$0	$0	$0	$0	$0	0%
—	0%	0	$0	$0	$0	$0	$0	$0	$0	$0	$0	$0	$0	0%
—	0%	0	$0	$0	$0	$0	$0	$0	$0	$0	$0	$0	$0	0%
—	0%	0	$0	$0	$0	$0	$0	$0	$0	$0	$0	$0	$0	0%
—	0%	0	$0	$0	$0	$0	$0	$0	$0	$0	$0	$0	$0	0%
—	0%	0	$0	$0	$0	$0	$0	$0	$0	$0	$0	$0	$0	0%
—	0%	0	$0	$0	$0	$0	$0	$0	$0	$0	$0	$0	$0	0%
—	0%	0	$0	$0	$0	$0	$0	$0	$0	$0	$0	$0	$0	0%
—	0%	0	$0	$0	$0	$0	$0	$0	$0	$0	$0	$0	$0	0%

Total Profit $0

Figure 6–8   Your discounted cash flow: status quo (EXCURVE; range name: DCFstatusquo).

Discounted Cash Flow: Status Quo				Range Name: DCFstatusquo	
Year	Operating Profit	Add Back Deprec.	Initial Cost	Total Cash Flow	Discount Factor 0.00%
			$0	$0	$0
___	$0	$0		$0	
___	$0	$0		$0	
___	$0	$0		$0	
___	$0	$0		$0	
___	$0	$0		$0	
___	$0	$0		$0	
___	$0	$0		$0	
___	$0	$0		$0	
___	$0	$0		$0	
___	$0	$0		$0	

minimize it.) If you insert 16 percent instead of 15 percent, the number below becomes −123,940. If you insert 14 percent, the number becomes 62,352. Therefore, 15 percent is correct.

The computer model has files for six different experience curve strategies and a composite that adds all the strategies you complete into one. They are pricing (growthpricing), sales (growthsales), promotion (growthpromotion), vertical integration (growthvalueadded), manufacturing/engineering (growthmfgeng), customer service/distribution (growthcsdist) and the composite (growthcomposite).

Following are the case history files for the pricing strategy.

Calculating a Pricing Strategy

Let's assume one of your markets is sensitive to price; you are in a position to absorb a loss for a few years; and you don't believe your competitors can or will match a price cut on your part. Let's further assume that if you lower your price from $400 to $270 for two years and then to $235 for another three years, you could increase your annual growth rate from 10 percent to 30 percent. Probably by the end of this five-year plan your competitors would be forced out of the market, at which time you would increase your price to $410. (Probably excessive numbers, but the theory is the same.)

Based on these assumptions, you can use the Excel file to determine what would be the DCF for this price-cutting strategy. As you can see in Figure 6–9, we inserted the above-mentioned growth rate (30 percent) in the growth rate column. The computer then calculates, based on the experience curve rate (determined back in Figure 6–1, what your costs of goods would be in subsequent years. As Figure 6–9 shows, costs for our hypothetical SBU would be driven from $232 in 2009 to $142.59 in 2019.

Because we are considering a price-cutting strategy here, we will keep all other costs the same as in the past on a per unit basis. For example, as shown in Figure 6–10, SBU has been spending $50 per unit on sales activity and plans to keep it at this level. Next we have inserted a sales price and estimated industry growth rate. This enables the computer to calculate SBUs operating profit and market share. As we see in Figure 6–10, market share increases from 25 percent to 58 percent.

We can now check on the financial soundness of this strategy. We go to Discounted Cash Flow: Price (range name: DCF-price) (see Figure 6–11), and insert the investment needed to execute this plan for the status quo plan, which is $2,000,000. In a pricing strategy such as this one, total investment and operating profit, rather than just incremental investment and operating profit resulting from the new strategy, is used in calculating DCF. This is because a price cut affects the previous base of business as well as any new business. For the other types of strategies only incremental investment and operating profit will be used on calculating DCF. Then we inserted non-cash

Figure 6–9 Estimated cost of goods experience—SBU pricing (CEXCURVE; range name: Growthpricing).

Estimated Future Cost of Goods Experience—SBU Pricing   Range name: Growthpricing

2010-2019

Component A: # per unit = 1 ; Component B: # per unit = 1 ; Component C (Outside supplier): # per unit = 2

Year	Growth Rate	# Units Produced	Cum Vol	Comp. A Exp. Curve 84.34% Units	Comp. A Cost 84.34%	Doubled	Comp. B Exp. Curve 87.36% Units	Comp. B Cost 87.36%	Doubled	Comp. C Exp. Curve 81.90% Units	Comp. C Cost 81.90%	Doubled	Total Cost	Doubled
2010	30%	2,533	11,436	11,436	$30.00	3	22,872	$58.00	3	15,436	$86.00	1	$232.00	3
2011	30%	3,293	13,969	13,969	$30.00	3	27,938	$58.00	3	17,969	$86.00	1	$232.00	3
2012	30%	4,281	17,263	17,263	$25.30	4	34,525	$50.67	4	21,263	$70.44	2	$197.08	4
2013	30%	5,566	21,544	21,544	$25.30	4	43,088	$50.67	4	25,544	$70.44	2	$197.08	4
2014	30%	7,235	27,110	27,110	$25.30	4	54,219	$50.67	4	31,110	$70.44	2	$197.08	4
2015	10%	7,959	34,345	34,345	$21.34	5	68,690	$44.26	5	38,345	$57.69	2	$180.30	5
2016	10%	8,755	42,304	42,304	$21.34	5	84,608	$44.26	5	46,304	$57.69	3	$167.56	5
2017	10%	9,630	51,059	51,059	$21.34	5	102,118	$44.26	5	55,059	$57.69	3	$167.56	5
2018	10%	10,593	60,689	60,689	$18.00	6	121,379	$38.67	6	64,689	$57.69	3	$167.56	5
2019	10%	11,653	71,283	71,283	$18.00	6	142,566	$38.67	6	75,283	$57.69	3	$153.03	6
			82,936	82,936			165,871			86,936	$47.25	4	$142.59	6

	Exp. Rate 84.34%		Exp. Rate 87.36%		Exp. Rate 81.90%		Exp. Rate 86.99%

Figure 6-10 Pricing strategy (CEXCURVE; range name: SBUpricing).

SBU   X
Plan   A

Pricing
Total Costs, Pricing, Share and Profit—SBU
(Units & Operating Income in Hundreds)

Exhibit 8
SBU Pricing
Range Name: SBUpricing

Year	Growth Rate	# Units Prod.	Cost of Goods	Sales	Prom.	CS/Dist.	Value Added	Mfg./Eng.	G/A	Total Costs	Sales Price	Oper. Profit	Ind. Growth	Share
2002		1,000	$329	$50	$20	$5	$0	$0	$20	$424	$400	($24,000)	10%	25%
2003	10%	1,100	$299	$50	$20	$5	$0	$0	$20	$394	$400	$6,408	10%	25%
2004	10%	1,210	$299	$50	$20	$5	$0	$0	$20	$394	$400	$7,049	10%	25%
2005	10%	1,331	$273	$50	$20	$5	$0	$0	$20	$368	$400	$42,118	10%	25%
2006	10%	1,464	$254	$50	$20	$5	$0	$0	$20	$349	$400	$74,148	10%	25%
2007	10%	1,611	$254	$50	$20	$5	$0	$0	$20	$349	$400	$81,563	10%	25%
2008	10%	1,772	$232	$50	$20	$5	$0	$0	$20	$327	$400	$129,324	10%	25%
2009	10%	1,949	$232	$50	$20	$5	$0	$0	$20	$327	$400	$142,256	10%	25%
2010	30%	2,533	$232	$50	$20	$5	$0	$0	$20	$327	$270	($144,400)	10%	30%
2011	30%	3,293	$197	$50	$20	$5	$0	$0	$20	$292	$270	($72,705)	10%	35%
2012	30%	4,281	$197	$50	$20	$5	$0	$0	$20	$292	$235	($244,363)	10%	41%
2013	30%	5,566	$197	$50	$20	$5	$0	$0	$20	$292	$235	($317,672)	10%	49%
2014	30%	7,235	$180	$50	$20	$5	$0	$0	$20	$275	$235	($291,618)	10%	58%
2015	10%	7,959	$168	$50	$20	$5	$0	$0	$20	$263	$410	$1,173,490	10%	58%
2016	10%	8,755	$168	$50	$20	$5	$0	$0	$20	$263	$410	$1,290,838	10%	58%
2017	10%	9,630	$168	$50	$20	$5	$0	$0	$20	$263	$410	$1,419,922	10%	58%
2018	10%	10,593	$153	$50	$20	$5	$0	$0	$20	$248	$410	$1,715,864	10%	58%
2019	10%	11,653	$143	$50	$20	$5	$0	$0	$20	$238	$410	$2,009,100	10%	58%

Total Profit $6,997,324

Figure 6–11   Discounted cash flow: Price (CEXCURVE; range name: DCFprice).

Discounted Cash Flow: Price   Range Name: DCFPrice

Year	Operating Profit	Add Back Deprec.	Initial Cost	Total Cash Flow	Discount Factor 16.00%
			$2,000,000	($2,000,000)	($48,972)
2007	($144,400)	$66,677		($77,723)	
2008	($72,705)	$66,677		($6,028)	
2009	($244,363)	$66,677		($177,686)	
2010	($317,672)	$66,677		($250,995)	
2011	($291,618)	$66,677		($224,941)	
2012	$1,173,490	$66,677		$1,240,167	
2013	$1,290,838	$66,677		$1,357,515	
2014	$1,419,922	$66,677		$1,486,599	
2015	$1,715,864	$66,677		$1,782,541	
2016	$2,009,100	$66,677		$2,075,777	

expenditures, in this case depreciation, and the computer calculates the DCF for the plan. In the case history, it is 16 percent.

The discounted cash flow rate is only 16 percent for this pricing strategy, just one point above the status quo of 15 percent. Unless you made a mistake in your calculations or want to make some changes in the strategy, this activity does not make financial sense. That is the value of these files. You keep trying different strategies until you obtain a good financial return.

You may have noticed that no tax was taken out of operating income. To calculate true DCF, you should go to EXCURVE.xls (range name DCFprice) and fill in your data as we have done in Figure 6–11. Because there is such a wide variation on how tax is calculated for various companies, this has not been included in the model.

What If . . . ?

Following are five additional strategies that you can experiment with by asking yourself what if I did this or that. You are looking for the one that gives you your best discounted case flow. The strategies are value added, promotion, sales, customer service/distribution and manufacturing/engineering. You should look at the case histories first on Cexcurve.xls and then go to Excurve.xls and fill in your data.

Value Added

The primary reason for vertical integration is to increase value added because the higher the value added, everything else being equal, the higher the ROI.

There are two ways to vertically integrate: backward ("upstream") and forward ("downstream"). If you are a paper manufacturer, an example of upstream integration is the growing of trees and of downstream, the purchase or development of retail stores that sell your paper. The major factor to consider in integration is margins (operating profit before taxes expressed as a percent of total sales or revenues). You normally want to go in the direction of the highest margins and they usually increase as you move closer to the end user of your product or service. If you integrate upstream, the product or service is normally more of a commodity and therefore price is a major factor and margins are small. Conversely, if you market your products to the retail trade, such as Reynolds Metals (Reynolds Wrap and a host of other consumer products), you can enjoy margins as high as 30 to 40 percent. However, you have to understand the business. DuPont decided to sell the core of their business—nylon and textiles—and became a "science company." I cannot find an explanation for the switch, but it has not gone very well for them. They moved from a market they knew and were strong in to a market they don't know that well and are not strong in. They were profitable the last two quarters, but their stock price is lower than it was seven years ago.

Recently, companies have become more prone to go vertical. Oracle Corporation bought Sun Microsystems to transform the company into a maker of software, computers, and computer components. Pepsi is buying distributors because they want more control over distribution. Boeing purchased Vought Aircraft Industries to add control over manufacturing and Apple bought P.A. Semi for their customized microprocessors.

Value added is the percent of the selling price that you add to cover your own activity. If you buy raw materials for $200 and fabricate them into a machine that you sell for $1,000, your value added is 80 percent. Therefore, the more you integrate, the higher your value added.

Now, returning to our case study of SBU X, it is estimated that by executing a vertical integration strategy and a slight reduction in price based on resulting cost savings, annual sales growth can be increased from the current 10 percent to 13 percent for five years and then back to 10 percent for the next five years. This is shown in the CEXCURVE.xls file "Estimated Future Cost of Goods Experience—Value Added" (range name: Growthvalueadded). This increased sales volume would lower costs of goods from $232 to $167.56 by 2019.

In the CEXCURVE, "Value Added Strategy" (range name: SBUvalueadded), the anticipated cost savings of $10 per unit for the years 2010 to 2013 and $15 for 2014 to 2019 are shown. Price has been decreased from $400 to $390 beginning in 2010 and to $385 in 2014. The financials for this strategy are shown in the Excel file "Discounted Cash Flow: Value Added" (range name: DCFvalueadded). The incremental DCF rate is 27 percent.

Promotion Strategy

Nobody does it better than Procter & Gamble. Although they usually launch with a superior product, it is the power of their advertising and sales promotion that makes them either one or two in market share in most of their markets. However, once again, you have to know what you are doing. Texas Instruments, a technology-driven company, tried three times to crack consumer markets (hand-held calculators, watches, and personal computers for the home) and failed miserably each time. After announcing they were getting out of consumer marketing, their stock increased $50 the next day.

Returning to our case study of SBU X, it is estimated that by executing a heavy promotion strategy, annual sales growth can be increased from the current 10 percent to 14 percent for five years and then back to 10 percent for the next five years. This is shown in the CEXCURVE file "Estimated Future Cost of Goods Experience—Promotion" (range name: Growthpromotion). This increased sales volume would lower costs of goods from $232 to $167.56 by 2019.

In the CEXCURVE file "Promotion Strategy" (range name: SBUpromotion), promotion expenditures per unit have been increased from the current $20 to $50 for the period 2010 to 2014 and dropped back to $20 for the period 2015 to 2019. The resulting share increase is from the current 25 percent to 30 percent in 2019.

This is one of the strategies behind the introduction of Fresca, the Coca-Cola Company soft drink. Fresca was the first successful non-sugar soft drink. Sugar accounts for over 50 percent of ingredient costs in a soft drink and consequently the Coca-Cola Company could afford a much higher per unit advertising expenditure on Fresca. The drink was very successful until the company had to change the formula due to the ban on cyclamates.

The financials for this strategy are shown in the Excel file "Discounted Cash Flow: Promotion" (range name: DCFpromotion). The incremental DCF rate is only 15 percent.

Sales Strategy

Maybe emphasis on sales is the direction to go, like IBM (consulting). Sales activity can be inserted into the Excel file. The range names are in the upper right-hand corner of the charts (growthsales, SBUsales, and DCFsales). In the case history, a growth rate increase from the current 10 percent to 16 percent is projected for five years. Sales expense has been increased from $50 to $100 per unit. Projected share increase is from 25 percent to 33 percent and the resulting incremental DCF is 12 percent.

Customer Service /Distribution Strategy

Disney, British Airways, and Marriott know the power of customer service. Fed Ex and Wal-Mart know the power of unique distribution.

This section is covered in the Excel file (range names: growthcsdist, SBUcsdist, and DCFcsdist) as well. In the case history, increased growth rate is projected from the current 10 percent to 13 percent for five years. Customer service/distribution costs are increased from $5 to $18 per unit. Share increases from 25 percent to 29 percent, and the DCF for this execution is estimated at 24 percent.

Manufacturing/Engineering Strategy

Here comes the better mousetrap; the best strategy of all if you can pull it off. Use the following ranges for your attempt to find a better mousetrap (range names: growthmfgeng,

SBUmfgeng, and DCFmfgeng). For SBU X, it is estimated that they will achieve the best DCF with an investment of $350,000 (too bad it isn't quite that simple). Growth rate increases to 14 percent and share to 29 percent. They are even able to reduce their manufacturing costs $12 per unit. The incremental DCF is 33 percent.

If you are considering developing a new product or service, these files will help you determine your project goals and with research, you can maintain close contact with your customers as the following company, a medical-device manufacturer, did. This company created a matrix to identify and weigh the importance of various features to different customer segments. It then tested trade-offs between product and things like price with various medical specialists who used the product in simulated clinical settings. That allowed the team to fine-tune the product well before launch for medical testing.[3]

Composite of Above Strategies

On the composite range names, all the previous strategies except for the pricing strategy are added together and we get the final results (range names: growthcomposite, SBUcomposite, and DCFcomposite). There's no need to add anything to growthcomposite because all its data is picked up from other ranges. On SBUcomposite, everything is picked up except the new sales price, the industry growth, and the beginning share. On DCFcomposite, one only has to insert the right DCF rate.

In the case history, the total growth rate is 30 percent for five years and then levels off at 10 percent for the remaining five. Cost of goods goes down from $232 in 2009 to $142.50 in 2019. Total costs, even with all this new activity, goes from

$424 in 2002 to just $213 in 2019. Market share increases to 58 percent (you own the market) and the incremental DCF is 30 percent.

The discounted cash flow of each strategy can be charted with Excel's charting function as seen in Figure 6–12. This is one of seven charts on the various strategies available on the CEXCURVE file.

For at least some of you, using the experience curve can give you great savings. For example, the computer chip industry is on a very high experience curve rate cost reduction, probably in the neighborhood of 50 percent. That means that every time you double your volume, your costs are 50 percent lower. Today you can hold in the palm of your hand a computer chip

Figure 6–12   Discounted cash flow by strategy (CEXCURVE; chart name: DCFfunctions).

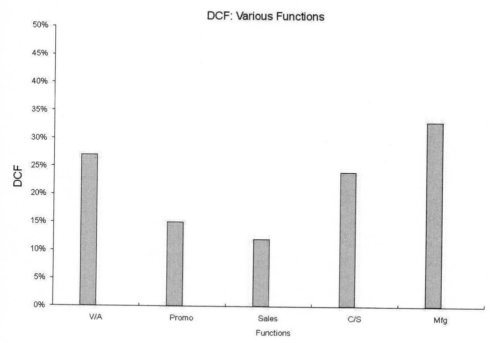

that has more power than a computer manufactured forty years ago that was so large it would have filled six to ten bedrooms. If the American automobile industry had pushed the experience curve similar to the computer industry, a Cadillac today would cost $50 and be able to drive around the world on one tank of gas.

The discounted cash flow rate for these various strategies has nothing to do with the feasibility or possible effectiveness that they would have in your market. They are just case histories showing how to calculate the results.

Following is a worksheet for your product/service plan. You can photocopy this one, or print out a copy from the Worksheets folder you downloaded. (Okay, one last time: www.amacombook.org/go/MarketingPlan4.) You can change my categories if appropriate, and you should probably not put in volume and share until after you go through the upcoming sales plan chapters (Chapters 12 and 13). By "type of mousetrap," I mean which of the four approaches discussed above is going to be your thrust.

Worksheet 6–1   Product/service plan: Objectives and strategies

Objectives

1. Type of mousetrap: _____

   _____

2. Volume/share: _____

   _____

3. Models/services: _____

   _____

4. New products/services: _____

   _____

Strategies

1. _____

   _____

2. _____

   _____

3. _____

   _____

4. _____

   _____

Notes

1. Marc Gunther, "Marriott Gets a Wake-Up Call," *Fortune*, July 6, 2009; http://money.cnn.com/2009/06/22/news/companies/marriott_hotels_makeover.fortune/?postversion=2009062508.

2. Kate Rockwood, "Rising Dough, Why Panera Bread Is on a Roll," *Fast Company*, October 2009; http://www.fastcompany.com/magazine/139/rising-dough.html.

3. Mike Gordon, Chris Musso, Eric Rebentisch, and Nisheeth Gupta, "The Path to Developing Successful New Products," *Wall Street Journal*, November 30, 2009; http://online.wsj.com/article/NA_WSJ_PUB:SB10001424052970203440104574400593760720388.html#articleTabs%3Darticle.

7 · Calculating Your Marketing Communications Budget

Some consultants or authors recommend that in certain industries, you dedicate a particular percent of sales for your marketing communications budget. I believe this is bad advice; you should not be spending the same amount as your competitors. In those markets that you are pushing, you should be spending more and in those markets where you are harvesting, you should be spending less. For example, your budget should be tied to your plans relative to market share objective, number of new products or services, market growth, plant or facility utilization, amount of sales transaction, importance to customer, premium or discounted pricing, relative quality, depth of line, and a standard versus custom brand.

Following are some formulas that you can use to factor in these components to calculate your budget. First, in Worksheet 7–1, you calculate your participant market factor, which is based on your total sales. Then you adjust this factor, based on the market objectives mentioned above, in Worksheets 7–2 through 7–11 to calculate your budget, as shown on Worksheet 7–12.

For example, Worksheet 7–2 factors in your market share objective. If your objective is less than 10 percent, you reduce your marketing communications budget (developed in the very first worksheet) to only 40 percent. If it is between 10 and 16.9 percent, you reduce it to only 70 percent. If it is between 17 and 24.9 percent, you reduce it to only 80 percent. However, if it you are going for a market share between 25 and 39.9 percent, you increase it by 1.20 percent and if over 40 percent, you double it.

You make these adjustments based on your various objectives on Worksheets 7–3 to 7–11 and insert the resulting budget figures on Worksheet 7–12. You add them up and then divide by the number of charts you used—and that is your marketing communications budget.

Worksheet 7–1   Participant's market factor

This worksheet enables you to calculate your participant market factor, the "base" budget number that you will use on all of the subsequent worksheets. Line 1 is the name of your company; line 2 your products or services; line 3 your current sales or a new sales target arrived at from the previous chapter as well as other chapters in the book.

1. Participant's market: _____

2. Product/service for this market: _____

3. Estimate of total sales for participant: _____

4. Divide line 3 by 750. This is your participant market factor: $ _____

You may want to plug this amount into each of the following worksheets where indicated now, before continuing with this chapter.

Worksheet 7–2   Factoring in your market share objective

This worksheet helps you calculate your budget if it were based solely on your market share objective.

1. Market share objective: _____% _____

2. Choose a multiplication factor based on your market share objective: _____

Objective	Multiplication Factor
0–9.9%	.40
10–16.9%	.70
17–24.9%	.80
25–39.9%	1.20
40% and over	2.00

3. Participant's market factor (from Worksheet 7–1): _____

4. Multiply line 2 by line 3: _____

Enter the budget amount from line 4 on line A in Worksheet 7–12.

Worksheet 7–3   Introducing a new product/service

Use this worksheet to calculate your budget as if it were based solely on new product/service considerations.

1. Total estimated sales of new product/service in market: _____

2. Company sales in new product/service market: _____

3. New product/service sales as a percent of total company sales: _____%

Share	Multiplication Factor
24.9% or less	.70
25%–39.9%	.80
40%–59.9%	1.40
60% and over	1.50

4. Choose a multiplication factor based on your percent of total: _____

5. Participant's market factor (from Worksheet 7–1): _____

6. Multiply line 4 by line 5: _____

Enter the amount from line 6 on line B in Worksheet 7–12.

Worksheet 7–4   Market growth

This worksheet will allow you to calculate your budget based on the estimated growth of your market.

1. Estimated total sales in market: _____

2. Estimated sales next year: _____

3. Percentage increase: _____%

Market growth	Multiplication Factor
No growth (less than 1%)	.80
Slow growth (1%–4.9%)	.90
Moderate growth (5%–11.9%)	1.20
Rapid growth (12% or more)	1.30

4. Choose your multiplication factor based on the rate of growth: _____

5. Participant's market factor (from Worksheet 7–1): _____

6. Multiply line 4 by line 5: _____

Enter the amount from line 6 on line C in Worksheet 7–12.

Worksheet 7–5   Plant utilization

This worksheet allows you to calculate your budget based on plant utilization.

1. Estimated plant utilization capacity: _____%

2. Choose a multiplication factor based on the figures below: _____

Capacity utilization	Multiplication Factor
Under 65.9%	1.25
65%–84.9%	1.10
85% and over	.80

3. Participant's market factor (from Worksheet 7–1): _____

4. Multiply line 2 by line 3: _____

Enter the amount from line 4 on line D in Worksheet 7–12.

Worksheet 7–6   Amount of typical sales transaction

Use this worksheet to calculate the budget based on the amount of a typical sales transaction.

1. Amount of typical sales transaction: $ _____

2. Choose a multiplication factor based on the figures below: _____

Typical sales transaction	Multiplication Factor
Under $100	1.70
$100–999	1.30
$1,000–9,999	1.20
$10,000–99,999	1.00
Over $100,000	.90

3. Participant's market factor (from Worksheet 7–1): _____

4. Multiply line 2 by line 3: _____

Enter the amount from line 4 on line E of Worksheet 7–12.

Worksheet 7–7   Importance to customer

Use this worksheet to calculate your marketing communications budget based on the importance or your product/service to the customer.

1. Percent of customer's total purchases: _____%

2. Choose your multiplication factor based on the chart below: _____

Percent of total purchases	Multiplication Factor
< 1%	1.35
1%–4.9%	1.00
5%–24.9%	.90
> 25%	.80

3. Participant's market factor (from Worksheet 7–1): _____

4. Multiply line 2 by line 3: _____

Enter the amount from line 4 on line F of Worksheet 7–12.

Worksheet 7–8   Premium or discounted pricing

This worksheet enables you to calculate your budget based on the type of pricing (premium or discounted pricing) you use.

1. Ranking of your price versus competition

   Low (discount) _____ Average _____ High (premium) _____

2. Choose a multiplication factor based on the price of your product/service: _____

Price of product/service	Multiplication Factor
Low or discounted	1.00
Average price	.80
High or premium	1.30

3. Participant's market factor (from Worksheet 7–1): _____

4. Multiply line 2 by line 3: _____

Enter the amount from line 4 on line G of Worksheet 7–12.

Worksheet 7–9   Relative quality

Use this worksheet to calculate your marketing communications budget based on the relative quality of your product or service.

1. Relative quality versus competition

   Lower _____ Average _____ Higher _____

2. Choose a multiplication factor based on your ranking in the chart below: _____

Quality ranking	Multiplication Factor
Lower quality	.85
Average quality	1.00
Higher quality	1.35

3. Participant's market factor (from Worksheet 7–1): _____

4. Multiply line 2 by line 3: _____

Enter the amount from line 4 on line H of Worksheet 7–12.

Worksheet 7–10 Depth of line

Use this worksheet to calculate the marketing communications budget based on the depth of line of your product or service.

1. Depth of line versus competition

   Narrow _____ Equal _____ Broader _____

2. Choose your multiplication factor from the chart below: _____

Depth of line	Multiplication Factor
Narrower	.90
Equal	1.00
Broader	1.30

3. Participant's market factor (from Worksheet 7–1): _____

4. Multiply line 2 by line 3: _____

Enter the amount from line 4 on line I of Worksheet 7–12.

Worksheet 7–11 Standard versus custom product/service

This worksheet enables you to calculate the impact of having a standard or a custom product or service.

1. Is your product/service standard or custom: _____

2. Choose the appropriate multiplication factor from the chart below: _____

Type of product/service	Multiplication Factor
Standard	1.10
Custom	.80

3. Participant's market factor (from Worksheet 7–1): _____

4. Multiply line 2 by line 3: _____

Enter the amount from line 4 on line J of Worksheet 7–12.

Worksheet 7–12 below should be all filled in now that you have reached the end of the chapter (unless you decided that a particular variable was not relevant to your particular product or service and so left that row blank). You should be easily able to add all the budgets and find the average.

Worksheet 7–12   Recap

---

1. Fill in amounts from the earlier worksheets:
   A. Market share $ _____
   B. New product/service $ _____
   C. Market growth $ _____
   D. Capacity utilization $ _____
   E. Amount of sales transaction $ _____
   F. Importance to customer $ _____
   G. Premium or discounted $ _____
   H. Relative quality $ _____
   I. Depth of line $ _____
   J. Standard or custom $ _____

2. Total $ _____

3. Divide your total in line 2 by the number of worksheets you used (_____) to find the recommended advertising budget: $ _____

Sales promotion should be about the same amount, and your public relations budget about a third of your advertising budget.

The amount on line 3 of Worksheet 7–12 is the recommended advertising budget, although you should compare this amount with the reach and frequency worksheet in Chapter 9, The Advertising Plan.

Source for the worksheets, with some adjustments, is PIMS and Cahners Publishing.

8 · Competitive Analysis

To be effective in marketing, you need to be competitive with your product or service, promotion, distribution, customer service, technology—just about anything you can think of. Even mighty Microsoft is failing with their mobile phone software, which is considered by many to have a boring interface and sluggish response time. In this chapter we offer a series of worksheets that will allow you to compare your company to the competition along many parameters. You are asked to score yourself on a scale of 1 to 10 in each of the worksheets below against your three major competitors.

You will not have "hard data" to make many of these assessments, but the better you know your industry and your competition, the more useful this competitive analysis will be. Some of the data can be obtained through research on your part (see Chapter 17, The Research Plan), and for some, you will just "wing it." Give it your best shot.

Where you find yourself weak, you need a plan to make yourself stronger. Where you excel, if it is considered a vital factor in the buying decision, these factors should be your basic thrust in your promotions.

You can make photocopies of these worksheets, or print them out from your downloaded Worksheets folder.

Worksheet 8–1 Product/service				
	SBU	#1 Comp.	#2 Comp.	#3 Comp.
Quality	___	___	___	___
Differentiation	___	___	___	___
Depth of line	___	___	___	___
Packaging	___	___	___	___
Relative price	___	___	___	___
Preference level	___	___	___	___
Trial rate	___	___	___	___
Repurchase rate	___	___	___	___
Compatibility	___	___	___	___
Ease of use	___	___	___	___

Quality is usually considered a vital factor, and is the reason for the success of Marriott Hotels, Coach, and Apple. Differentiation is also critical, otherwise why would customers buy your product or use your service instead of the competition's, unless you are relying on discounted pricing. Depth of line, which is the number of products or services you offer, is also important for maximum profit, and is a big part of the strategy of Coca-Cola and McDonald's. If you don't know your trial rate and your repurchase rate, you should be able to get that information from a benchmark research study or perhaps from other departments in your organization. It's important information to have, and will come up again in Chapter 13, The Sales Plan: Future Sales.

Worksheet 8–2 asks you to rate yourself on manufacturing.

Although manufacturing is not part of marketing, you need the right resources on which to build a marketing plan for a product. Value added, which is a vertical or horizontal

Worksheet 8–2   Manufacturing

	SBU	#1 Comp.	#2 Comp.	#3 Comp.
Value added	___	___	___	___
Manufacturing costs	___	___	___	___
Productivity	___	___	___	___
Capacity utilization	___	___	___	___
Labor costs	___	___	___	___
Raw material availability	___	___	___	___
Product/process protection	___	___	___	___
Pushing experience curve	___	___	___	___
CAD/CAM	___	___	___	___

integration strategy such as Cisco's expansion into other markets, and pushing the experience curve (as Japanese industries are so well known for doing) can lower your cost of goods and leave more for marketing.

Worksheet 8–3 asks you to look at how well you stack up against your competition in terms of promotion.

Worksheet 8–3   Promotion

	SBU	#1 Comp.	#2 Comp.	#3 Comp.
Advertising expenditures	___	___	___	___
Sales promotion expenditures	___	___	___	___
Sales support expenditures	___	___	___	___
Public relations expenditures	___	___	___	___
Creativity	___	___	___	___
Brand/company awareness level	___	___	___	___
Brand/company "would consider" level	___	___	___	___

Brand/company "intend

   to buy" level   ___   ___   ___   ___

The previous chapter on your marketing communication budget provides you with charts to help you calculate your budget for advertising, sales promotion, and public relations. You have the reach and frequency calculation spreadsheet for advertising in the chapter on advertising (Chapter 9); the one for trade shows, etc., is in the chapter on sales promotion (Chapter 10). The research chapter (Chapter 17) will tell you how to use a benchmark study to obtain your awareness level, your "would consider" and "intend to buy" levels, among your target audience, as well as how to measure the creativity of your advertisements. Again, a benchmark study will answer these questions for you.

You don't have to outspend competition to win, just more effective marketing. However, if one or more of your competitors are outspending you and have a powerful creative department, you should stop everything and determine how you are going to fight back. Do you alter the product or service for greater appeal and/or obtain a more effective creative department?

Worksheet 8–4 will help you determine your competitive score in terms of retailing.

Worksheet 8–4 Retailing			
	SBU	**#1 Comp.**	**#2 Comp.**	**#3 Comp.**
Merchandising	___	___	___	___
Location of outlets	___	___	___	___
Appearance of outlets	___	___	___	___
Warmth of employees	___	___	___	___
Markups	___	___	___	___

Markdowns	___	___	___	___
Inventory turnover	___	___	___	___
Available capital	___	___	___	___
Convenience of shopping	___	___	___	___
Training of employees	___	___	___	___

If you are into retailing, you should take a trip to see Bloomingdale's in New York City. That is really a fun place to shop. You should also take a tour of Wal-Mart's home office or read about them because they understand the whole world of retailing better than any other company. In the past, their only weak spot was employee relations, but now they are providing more benefits to their employees.

Worksheet 8–5   Distribution/customer service

	BSU	#1 Comp.	#2 Comp.	#3 Comp.
Extent of served market coverage	___	___	___	___
Shelf space or dealer inventory	___	___	___	___
Distribution costs	___	___	___	___
Quality/expertise of trade channels	___	___	___	___
Inventory costs	___	___	___	___
Technical service	___	___	___	___
Technology	___	___	___	___
Databases	___	___	___	___
Capital	___	___	___	___
Resources				
Immediate customer satisfaction	___	___	___	___
End user satisfaction	___	___	___	___
Computerization	___	___	___	___

If your competition has more outlets than you do, their marketing costs per outlet will be less than yours and their entire cost structure will probably be more favorable. We have talked about customer service before and will again later, but remember, keeping a customer only costs about a fifth as much as acquiring a new one. The CEO who calls all her customers to ask how she can improve her service to them has an extremely high customer retention rate.

Worksheet 8-6 asks you to score yourself against the competition in terms of your sales force. Remember, these worksheets are very general, meant to help you home in on what your company is doing well—and where it is falling short.

Worksheet 8-6   Sales force

	SBU	#1 Comp.	#2 Comp.	#3 Comp.
Sales costs	___	___	___	___
Experience of sales personnel	___	___	___	___
Sales per sales call	___	___	___	___
Net margin per sales call	___	___	___	___
Closure rate	___	___	___	___
Time management	___	___	___	___
Salaries/bonuses	___	___	___	___
Sales training	___	___	___	___
Turnover	___	___	___	___
Communications	___	___	___	___
Expertise of sales managers	___	___	___	___
Sales aids	___	___	___	___

One of your most important marketing objectives should be to have the highest sales closer rate in the market. You can calculate your own internally and with a little investigation obtain competitive rates. You should always have a debriefing session with the prospect after the presentation. This enables you to find the pluses and minuses of your own team as well as hear the attributes of your competitors' sales talk. Once you know your own closure rate, you want to set a higher objective for the following year and your strategy should be some form of sales training.

Worksheet 8–7 asks you to evaluate your company in terms of research and development. If your company is not investing in its future, it probably won't have a very good one.

Worksheet 8–7 Research and development				
	SBU	#1 Comp.	#2 Comp.	#3 Comp.
R & D (% of sales)	——	——	——	——
New products/services last 2 years	——	——	——	——
Success of introductions	——	——	——	——
New uses/flankers last 2 years	——	——	——	——
Marketing-driven versus product-driven	——	——	——	——
New products/services (last 5 years) as % of sales	——	——	——	——

The key factor here is the number of new products/services in the last two years. Research indicates that about 70 percent of markets start to deteriorate within three years. The company with the highest percent of new items is usually the winner.

After you complete these worksheets, you will know what you do well against the competition, and where you need to pick up the pace. You will have the parameters you need for setting up your marketing objectives.

9 · The Advertising Plan

There are four separate aspects to an advertising plan that you must consider, as shown in Figure 9–1. You normally develop your two strategies and two plans *before* you write your objectives. We will discuss objectives at the end of the chapter.

Figure 9–1 Components of an advertising plan.

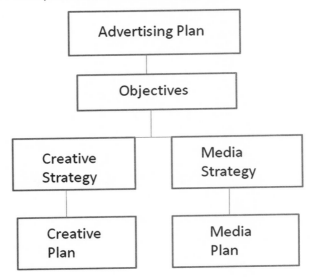

Let's start with the creative strategy. The creative strategy does not write the ad, but gives you guidance for developing the advertising and serves as a research tool to test whether your communications are on target. The creative strategy is normally written by the creative people in the advertising department, but it applies to all your communications to the customer. In Chapter 4 we talked about customer analysis, and it's vital that the analysis be done *before* you write your creative strategy.

The following eight statements express the creative strategy governing a successful outreach program warning the general public about the dangers of melanoma:

1. Objective: Encourage people to avoid sunburn.
2. Target: Teen sun worshippers.
3. Buying decision: Teens, moms, manufacturers, health professionals, clubs, schools.
4. Purpose: Use SPF 15+.
5. Promise teens: Be more attractive to the opposite sex.
   Promise moms: It's safe to stay in the sun longer.
   Promise manufacturers: Increased sales.
6. Support: SPF 15+ blocks most harmful rays (ACS, authority).
7. Personality: Healthy, effective, savvy, fun, contemporary.
8. Timing: Pre- and early tanning season (some continuous).

Notice that there are different selling lines for different targets—one for the end user (teens), one for the buyer (mom), and one for the trade. The original selling line for teens was, "It keeps you alive." Through research they discovered this did not turn teens on. Research revealed the clincher was, "Be more attractive to the opposite sex."

A few years ago, I did some consulting work for a privately held major stock brokerage company. Its promotional approach appeared to be off target, and when I told the managers this, they stated that the chairman of the board really liked the advertising campaign. In fact, he had each ad framed in his office. The chairman was then called into the meeting to hear the reasons the promotional activity should be canceled. He replied that there was a misunderstanding of the objective of the advertising campaign. He compared it to a United Technologies campaign. The United Technologies campaign says nothing about the product or service but addresses various issues that the company believes would be of interest to the reader. Each time a new ad appears, the company gets thousands of requests for reprints. The basic thrust for one ad that received over 10,000 requests for reprints made reference to the common phrase "my girl." The ad was addressed to males, and it queried why, when somebody called, males would say, get back to my girl, or call my girl for this, or have my girl do that. The copy went on to say, "Doesn't that girl have a name? Mary? Sue? Joanne? Then why don't you refer to her as Mary, Sue, or Joanne?"

I asked the chairman if he was familiar with the Boeing campaign featuring the 767s. The chairman replied that yes indeed, he was familiar with that campaign, and it was another example of what he was trying to do. He referred to this type of activity as "selling image." The problem here is that neither United Technologies or Boeing is selling image. What they are selling is their stock. And his company had no stock to sell.

The reason I bring up this story is to illustrate a common mistake in communications: that image in itself sells something. If by image you are referring to AFLAC's duck, then you are on target. However, if by image you are referring to your company or corporation, remember that the only time people buy companies is when they buy stock. At all other times they are buying a product or service.

As discussed in Chapter 4, Customer Analysis, you always want to lead your communications with a benefit and then support it with the features of your product or service. Figure 9–2 is a reproduction of an ad for Memorial Sloan-Kettering Cancer Center. It is a very unusual presentation of a letter addressed to Cancer, "Cancer, You said I'd never bear children. My daughter says you're wrong." That's a powerful headline. (Another thing I like about the ad is that they didn't use a fashion model.)

Figure 9–3 is a reproduction of an ad for Intuit Quick-Books. It's not a fancy ad, but I believe it appeals to every small business owner or manager. With a photo of business papers all over the floor, the headline reads, "Get your business off the ground." Quick and to the point.

Figure 9–4 is a reproduction of an ad for Chubb Insurance. Most insurance ads I see lead with the features of the policies. Not this one. As the canoe and man is about to fall off a falls, the headline reads, "Who insures you doesn't matter. Until it does."

I hope you noticed that on all three of the above ads, you just have to read the headline to get the benefit. Now look at the ad in Figure 9–5, which is like so many I see. The headline is, "You say obsessive like it's a bad thing." Please tell me what they are selling here, because I don't know. If you read the body copy, they do actually tell you what they are talking about, but always remember that only 10 percent of the people who read the headline read the body copy. (This statistic is based on several readership research studies conducted through the years.)

When you are able to develop an effective campaign, you should stick with it. I don't understand why United Airlines no longer uses their selling line, "Fly the friendly skies of United"

(text continues on page 124)

Figure 9–2   Ad for Memorial Sloan-Kettering Cancer Center.

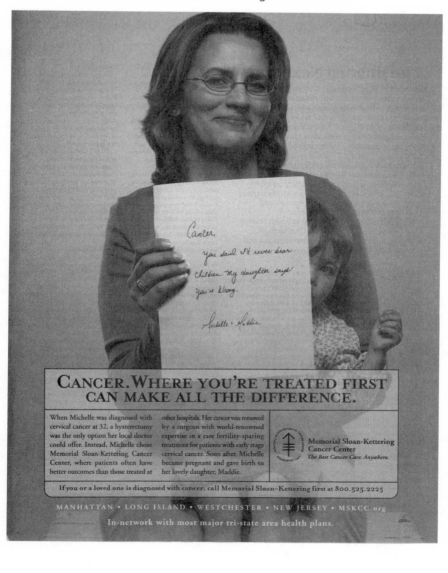

Figure 9–3   Ad for Intuit QuickBooks.

Figure 9–4   Ad for Chubb Insurance.

Figure 9–5   Ad for Ford Taurus.

with the beautiful accompanying music, in their advertising. It used to have the highest awareness level of any campaign. At least the pilots know better, because they still say, "Thanks for flying the friendly skies." The problem probably was that the creative people who developed the campaign thought they were not doing their job if they didn't come up with a new story. Well, I can't tell you what United is now saying in their ads. Can you tell me? See how memorable?

In your campaign, each of your ads should say basically the same thing. A common mistake is for a company to run an ad on let's say manufacturing one month and something totally different the next. How on earth does that happen? Well, the creative people say, "Hmmm, what haven't we talked about for a while? Oh, I know, let's now run an ad about our sales team." That is not the way to obtain maximum awareness.

The advantages of advertising is that it is the best tool for building awareness; television is an excellent reach medium; radio a good frequency medium; print a good rifle approach; outdoor offers the lowest cost per thousand; and the Internet can probably do all the above. The disadvantages are it takes a long time to work; it can be costly; and there is a lot of bad creativity.

You are about to write your creative strategy, so keep in mind that it:

1. Defines target audience in demographic as well as psychographic terms.
2. Formulates major benefits or positioning of product or service, along with copy points.
3. Does not "write" the ad, but provides *direction* for writing an effective ad.
4. Must provide sufficient direction to allow evaluation of ads and ad campaigns in all media.

Following is a worksheet you can use to write your creative strategy; photocopy this or print out a copy from your folder of downloaded worksheets.

Worksheet 9–1   Creative strategy

1. Objective: _____

_____

2. Target: _____

_____

3. Benefits: _____

_____

4. Features: _____

_____

5. Personality: _____

_____

6. Timing: _____

_____

After you complete your creative strategy, you should give a copy (hand-delivery is best, but e-mail will do) to everyone who communicates with the customer.

Media Strategy

In your media strategy, you want to describe how you are going to reach each individual in the purchase process. You may need some research to find out how each one obtains their news or communicates with others. Most individuals use more than one media, but if you're going after executives, it may be newspapers or certain magazines. For mom and dad, it may be television or radio. For the younger generation, it may be the Internet, cell phones, or TV. Mediabrands, an ad-buying unit of the Interpublic Group, just introduced a new unit called Geomentum. Geomentum plans to be able to allocate your ad budget among the 40,000 ZIP codes in the United States, some-times zeroing in on even smaller areas, like a city block.

Outdoor advertising gives you the lowest cost per thousand (CPM), with the national average being about $1.80 per thousand viewers. You can have thirty-sheet posters or painted bulletins, which are even larger. The New Jersey Nets recently bought a painted bulletin right outside of Madison Square Garden so that Madison Square Garden management could see the ad right outside of their windows—funny, and effective. The Knicks are no doubt fuming.

Outdoor advertising can be very effective if used correctly. Keep your message to between four and six words, in huge type. Most advertisers do not do this and it is impossible to read their message as you zoom by in your car. Posters are bought by the number of showings, with "a 100# showing" meaning that the gross number of impressions will be equal to the population of the city or area. That doesn't mean every person will see one of your posters because many people, who drive or walk by daily in certain areas, will see one of your posters several times. But the takeaway message is that outdoor delivers a very high frequency of viewers.

If your selling line incorporates full-color artwork or photography, you may want to consider mass circulation magazines, as long as they reach your target audience. Magazines are losing circulation due to all the activity on the Internet, so you now can get a good price break on your ad. Most magazines offer regional buys, so you don't have to be national to participate. Magazine advertising also enables you to have a Starch report, which is an inexpensive way to have your ad critiqued. Starch reports are discussed in Chapter 17, The Research Plan.

If your selling line includes sound, radio could be a good choice. Radio is a frequency medium, reaching a relatively small group many times. Stations have good research on their audiences, so if you can match up your target, it could be a go.

Newspapers, like magazines, are losing circulation. I take three daily papers, the local one plus the *Wall Street Journal* and the *New York Times*. However, there is just one other house on the block that has a paper delivered. Although young people are not into newspapers, they still can be an effective advertising medium if your target is business executives or you are selling retail. If you're going to run a newspaper campaign, you always want to talk to the editorial people first about having them give you some free publicity in a news article about your product or service. Ironically, you will probably get more feedback from the news article than your ads.

Television is the most effective advertising medium because it combines sight and sound, but it's expensive. However, like newspapers and magazines, rates are coming down due to all the action on the Internet, including programs, movies, and advertising. In fact, some of the local stations will shoot your commercial for you at a very reasonable rate. It won't compare with those produced by the commercial production houses, but if your story is simple, it may work. Don't overlook ten-second ID commercials. You can have them produced by the pros for a fraction of the cost of a thirty-second spot. A client of mine in San Diego was a local potato chip manufacturer who was competing against Granny Goose potato chips. I came up with the idea of a talking potato chip and had the ID shot in Hollywood. It kept my client competitive with his national competition.

You also want to check your advertising "weight." That means you will have to look into reach and frequency. Frequency is the number of times you reach the same individual (and past advertising research states the minimum should be five; the optimal range is between five and ten). The period of time you have to reach your minimum varies by media. For outdoor, daily newspapers, radio, television, and the Internet, it's a month; for weekly magazines it's three months; and for monthly magazines, a year.

Reach is the percent of your target audience that you reach at least once. When we get into your advertising plan's objectives, as we will later, you may have an awareness objective of 50 percent of the target audience. If that is true, you would need a reach figure of approximately 70 percent, because not all of your target will remember your ad.

The equation for reach and frequency is as follows:

$$\text{Gross number of impressions} = \text{reach} \times \text{frequency}$$

Divide both sides by reach.

$$\frac{\text{Gross number of impressions}}{\text{reach}} = \frac{\text{reach} \times \text{frequency}}{\text{reach}}$$

Reach cancels out on the right-hand side and the equation becomes

$$\frac{\text{Gross number of impressions}}{\text{reach}} = \text{frequency}$$

You will see how this works in the media plan.

Media Plan

Following are two of the four schedules in the reach and frequency case history.

Schedule 1 (the upper half of Figure 9–6) consists of fourteen insertions in four magazines, delivering a frequency of 4.57 (second to last column on the right) and a reach of only 32

Figure 9–6 Media analysis: Reach and frequency, CPM, and total cost; schedules 1 and 2 (CRF; range name: Schedule1&2).

Media Analysis: Reach & Frequency, CPM, and Total Cost

Range Name: Schedule 1 & 2

Schedule Number 1
SIC# 2345,6718,4334,6678
Target Number 500,000

#	Publicat.	Total Aud	Total Target Aud	Cost Per Unit	CPM Target	# Insert.	Gross Impres. #	Non-Duplic. (%)	Reach #	%	Cum Gross Imp.	Cum Reach	Cum Freq Target	Cum Total Cost
1	Mod. Eng.	100,000	75,000	$10,000	$133.33	4	300,000	100%	75,000	15%	300,000	75,000	4.00	$40,000
2	Eng. Dig.	70,000	50,000	$8,000	$160.00	4	200,000	67%	33,500	22%	500,000	108,500	4.61	$72,000
3	Eng. Mgm.	50,000	35,000	$7,800	$222.86	3	105,000	67%	23,450	26%	605,000	131,950	4.59	$95,400
4	CAD	50,000	40,000	$5,000	$125.00	3	120,000	67%	26,800	32%	725,000	158,750	4.57	$110,400
5					$0.00		0		0	32%	725,000	158,750	4.57	$110,400
6					$0.00		0		0	32%	725,000	158,750	4.57	$110,400
7					$0.00		0		0	32%	725,000	158,750	4.57	$110,400
8					$0.00		0		0	32%	725,000	158,750	4.57	$110,400
9					$0.00		0		0	32%	725,000	158,750	4.57	$110,400
10					$0.00		0		0	32%	725,000	158,750	4.57	$110,400
Total		270,000	200,000	$30,800	$154.00	14	725,000	79%	158,750	32%	725,000	158,750	4.57	$110,400

Reach 32%
Frequency 4.57
Cost $110,400
CPM $154.00

Schedule Number 2
SIC# 2345,6718,4334,6678
Target Number 500,000

#	Publicat.	Total Aud	Total Target Aud	Cost Per Unit	CPM Target	# Insert.	Gross Impres. #	Non-Duplic. (%)	Reach #	%	Cum Gross Imp.	Cum Reach	Cum Freq Target	Cum Total Cost
1	Cad	50,000	40,000	$5,000	$125.00	6	240,000	100%	48,000	8%	240,000	48,000	6.00	$30,000
2	Mod. Eng.	100,000	75,000	$10,000	$133.33	6	450,000	67%	58,250	18%	690,000	94,250	7.65	$90,000
3					$0.00		0		0	18%	690,000	94,250	7.65	$90,000
4					$0.00		0		0	18%	690,000	94,250	7.65	$90,000
5					$0.00		0		0	18%	690,000	94,250	7.65	$90,000
6					$0.00		0		0	18%	690,000	94,250	7.65	$90,000
7					$0.00		0		0	18%	690,000	94,250	7.65	$90,000
8					$0.00		0		0	18%	690,000	94,250	7.65	$90,000
9					$0.00		0		0	18%	690,000	94,250	7.65	$90,000
10					$0.00		0		0	18%	690,000	94,250	7.65	$90,000
Total		150,000	115,000	$15,000	$138.43	12	690,000	78%	94,250	18%	690,000	94,250	7.65	$90,000

Reach 18%
Frequency 7.65
Cost $90,000
CPM $138.43

percent (fifth column from the right). The information on how the number of times you reach the same individual comes from either the media itself or media research companies. If you are working with an advertising agency, the agency will supply this data.

Schedule 1 is clearly a weak schedule, so let's go to schedule 2. This one consists of twelve insertions in two of the magazines. This increases your frequency to 7.65, but the reach drops to just 18 percent. Now we will go to schedules 3 and 4, shown in Figure 9-7, from the same Excel file, to see if we can do better.

In schedule 3, we have the same magazines as in schedule 1, but the number of insertions has been increased to twenty-four. This gives us a frequency of 7.56, but only increases the reach to 32 percent. On schedule 4, we have added two more magazines and kept the insertions at twenty-four. This gives us a frequency of 5.30 and the reach increases to 44 percent. This is not a bad schedule if your objective is a relatively low awareness goal of say around 30 percent. If your objective is higher, then you have to increase the number of magazines you are using or add another type of media.

To give you an idea of how you might do, use your downloaded file "RF.xlw," and fill in the data for a magazine ad distribution schedule that you might want to try. Only fill in your data where you see blue lines or zeros. Although only the first two schedules are shown in Figure 9-8, the electronic file allows four variations, as you saw in Figures 9-6 and 9-7 above.

The above media analysis file can also be used for radio, TV, and even the Internet. You just insert the number of spots in place of the number of insertions.

Outdoor advertising has the lowest CPM, only $1.80 to reach a thousand people. Mass audience magazines, such as *People*, command the second lowest at $3.00. Next comes radio

(text continues on page 136)

Figure 9–7 Media analysis: Reach and frequency, CPM, and total cost; schedules 3 and 4 (CRF; range name: Schedule3_&4).

Schedule Number 3

Target Number   SIC# 2345,6718.4334,6678   500,000

Range Name: Schedule 3 & 4

#	Publicat.	Total Aud.	Total Target Aud.	Cost Per Unit	CPM Target	# Insert.	Gross # Impres.	Non-Duplic. (%)	Reach Reach #	%	Cum Gross Imp.	Cum, Reach	Freq. Target	Cum Total Cost
1	Mod. Eng.	100,000	75,000	$10,000	$133.33	6	450,000	100%	75,000	15%	450,000	75,000	6.00	$60,000
2	Eng. Dig.	70,000	50,000	$8,000	$160.00	6	300,000	67%	33,500	22%	750,000	108,500	6.91	$108,000
3	Eng. Mgm.	50,000	35,000	$7,800	$222.86	6	210,000	67%	23,450	26%	960,000	131,950	7.28	$154,800
4	CAD	50,000	40,000	$5,000	$125.00	6	240,000	67%	26,800	32%	1,200,000	158,750	7.56	$184,800
5					$0.00		0		0	32%	1,200,000	158,750	7.56	$184,800
6					$0.00		0		0	32%	1,200,000	158,750	7.56	$184,800
7					$0.00		0		0	32%	1,200,000	158,750	7.56	$184,800
8					$0.00		0		0	32%	1,200,000	158,750	7.56	$184,800
9					$0.00		0		0	32%	1,200,000	158,750	7.56	$184,800
10							0		0	32%	1,200,000	158,750	7.56	$184,800
Total		270,000	200,000	$30,800	$154.00	24	1,200,000	79%	158,750	32%	1,200,000	158,750	7.56	$184,800

Reach   32%
Frequency   7.56
Cost $184,800
CPM $154.00

Schedule Number 4

SIC# 2345,6718.4334,6678

#	Publicat.	Target Number Total Aud.	Total Target Aud.	Cost Per Unit	CPM Target	# Insert.	Gross # Impres.	Non-Duplic. (%)	Reach Reach #	%	Cum Gross Imp.	Cum, Reach	Freq. Target	Cum Total Cost
1	Mod. Eng.	100,000	75,000	$10,000	$133.33	4	300,000	100%	75,000	15%	300,000	75,000	4.00	$40,000
2	Eng. Dig.	70,000	50,000	$8,000	$160.00	4	200,000	67%	33,500	22%	500,000	108,500	4.61	$72,000
3	Eng. Mgm.	50,000	35,000	$7,800	$222.86	4	140,000	67%	23,450	26%	640,000	131,950	4.85	$103,200
4	CAD	50,000	40,000	$5,000	$125.00	4	160,000	67%	26,800	32%	800,000	158,750	5.04	$123,200
5	CAM	60,000	38,000	5,500	$144.74	4	152,000	67%	25,460	37%	952,000	184,210	5.17	$145,200
6	Exec. Eng.	150,000	55,000	$10,000	$181.82	4	220,000	67%	36,850	44%	1,172,000	221,060	5.30	$185,200
7					$0.00		0		0	44%	1,172,000	221,060	5.30	$185,200
8					$0.00		0		0	44%	1,172,000	221,060	5.30	$185,200
9					$0.00		0		0	44%	1,172,000	221,060	5.30	$185,200
10					$0.00		0		0	44%	1,172,000	221,060	5.30	$185,200
Total		480,000	293,000	$46,300	$158.02	24	1,172,000	75%	221,060	44%	1,172,000	221,060	5.30	$185,200

Target Number 500,000

Reach	44%
Frequency	5.30
Cost	$185,200
CPM	$158.02

Figure 9–8 Your media analysis: Range and frequency schedules 1 and 2 (RF; range name: Schedule1&2).

Media Analysis
Costs, CPM, Reach & Frequency
Range Name: Schedule 1 & 2

Schedule # ___
Target #

Publicat.	Total Aud.	Total Target Aud.	Cost Per Unit	CPM Target insert. #	Gross Impres. #	Non-Duplic. (%)	Reach #	Reach %	Cum Gross Imp.	Cum Reach	Cum Freq. Target	Cum Total Cost
				$0.00	0		0	0%	0	0	0.00	$0
				$0.00	0		0	0%	0	0	0.00	$0
				$0.00	0		0	0%	0	0	0.00	$0
				$0.00	0		0	0%	0	0	0.00	$0
				$0.00	0		0	0%	0	0	0.00	$0
				$0.00	0		0	0%	0	0	0.00	$0
				$0.00	0		0	0%	0	0	0.00	$0
				$0.00	0		0	0%	0	0	0.00	$0
				$0.00	0		0	0%	0	0	0.00	$0
	0	0	$0	$0.00	0	0%	0	0%	0	0	0.00	$0

Reach   0%
Frequency 0.00
Cost $0
CPM $0.00

Media Analysis
Costs, CPM, Reach & Frequency

Publicat.	Total Aud.	Total Target Aud.	Cost Per Unit	CPM Target	# Insert.	Gross # Impres.	Non-Duplic. (%)	Reach #	%	Cum Gross Imp.	Cum Reach	Freq. Target	Cum Total Cost
	—	—	—	$0.00	—	0	—	0	0%	0	0	0.00	$0
	—	—	—	$0.00	—	0	—	0	0%	0	0	0.00	$0
	—	—	—	$0.00	—	0	—	0	0%	0	0	0.00	$0
	—	—	—	$0.00	—	0	—	0	0%	0	0	0.00	$0
	—	—	—	$0.00	—	0	—	0	0%	0	0	0.00	$0
	—	—	—	$0.00	—	0	—	0	0%	0	0	0.00	$0
	—	—	—	$0.00	—	0	—	0	0%	0	0	0.00	$0
	—	—	—	$0.00	—	0	—	0	0%	0	0	0.00	$0
	—	—	—	$0.00	—	0	—	0	0%	0	0	0.00	$0
	0	0	$0	$0.00	0	0	0%	0	0%	0	0	0.00	$0

Reach	0%
Frequency	0.00
Cost	$0
CPM	$0.00

at $3.50 for a thirty-second commercial, followed by television at $6.00 for an early evening spot. However, TV can be expensive because it takes about fifteen spots per week for four weeks to obtain a frequency of 4—but the reach is around 80 percent. Newspapers are next most expensive at a CPM of $9.00, and trade magazines for men top our list at $12.00.

Creative Plan

The creative plan—not the creative strategy—is the actual advertising itself. Lead with the benefit, supported by the features. As I said in an earlier chapter, when it leaves the factory, it's called lipstick; when it is bought by the customer, it's called hope. In print advertising, the features belong in the body copy. Don't use reverse type or it will cut your readership by up to 80 percent. Try not to be too cute. Sometimes it's a problem understanding what the gecko says in the Geico television ads.

You want to test your ads or communications at various junctures, as shown in Figure 9–9, which shows a flow chart of the creative development process.

It seems clear to me that much advertising is pretty close to worthless. It's a wise investment of research dollars to be sure you are on target.

A management tool you may want to consider for your entire marketing team comes from an article in the Raleigh, North Carolina, *News & Observer* about McKinney, an advertising agency in Durham, North Carolina. Management felt it was important that employees run into one another and chat, as the average conversation can quickly turn into a creative epiphany. As a result, the mailroom and mailboxes now lie adjacent to a spacious café where employees gather to get a cup of coffee, grab a bite to eat, or catch up on the latest quirky news

Figure 9–9   Creative development testing timeline.

Creative Development

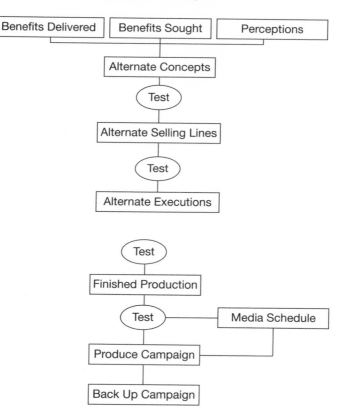

posted on a nearby magnetic board. But the café is not just for eating. An enormous white onyx table stretches the length of the room and has hosted everything from Mellow Mushroom pizza parties to exquisite catered events. Additional seating nearby and officewide Wi-Fi gives "McKinneyites" a chance to work wherever they are the most productive. And in many cases, it's in between conversations, right by the mailroom.[1] This approach could make your entire marketing team become closer and work better together.

Objectives and Strategies

Following is a worksheet for your advertising plan objectives and strategies. Photocopy this or print out a copy from your downloaded Worksheets folder. You can write over my terminology, but I inserted those categories to give you an idea what you should be measuring for.

Worksheet 9–2   Advertising plan: Objectives and strategies

Objectives

1. Awareness: _____

_____

2. Recall: _____

_____

3. Reach and frequency: _____

_____

4. _____

_____

Strategies

1. _____

_____

2. _____

_____

3. _____

_____

4. _____

_____

Note

1. Alli Soule, "Mailroom, Café Foster Chats," *News & Observer*, July 26, 2009.

10 · The Sales Promotion Plan

There are many types of sales promotion. Following are the major ones.

- Price deals
- Coupons
- Samples
- Premiums
- POP (point of purchase)

- Sweepstakes/contests
- Promotions
- Brochures
- Direct mail
- Trade shows

Let's take a look at them one by one.

Price Deals

The advantages of price deals are:

1. They can induce customers to try the product or service.
2. They can establish a purchase pattern.
3. They should increase sales.
4. They may neutralize competitive promotions.

The disadvantages of price deals are:

1. They don't build loyalty.
2. They don't reverse a declining sales trend.
3. They won't change "non-acceptance" of a brand.

When you discount your price, make it a surprise; save discounts until your supplier does something special. Don't use promotional discounts to sell in, but to sell through and position against the right type of customer.

Following is a chart that shows who buys your discounted merchandise.

	Regular merchandise	Discounted merchandise
Loyal buyers	41%	13%
Buyers loyal to competition	19%	24%
Not loyal to any brand	24%	21%
"Deal" buyers	16%	42%

Notice that 42 percent of the deal merchandise is bought by deal buyers, who most of the time will leave you as soon as you pull the promotion. The ideal promotion is one that is designed to attract the "not loyal to any brand" and "loyal to competition." Usually a bigger than average discount will entice these two groups.

Coupons

Coupons can be an effective promotional tool. I buy all my office supplies, including electronic gear, from the local Office-Max, because they mail me $10- and $20-off coupons every other week. I also buy all my books at Barnes & Noble because they e-mail me similar coupons every few weeks. Try to be unique for maximum impact. A local car dealer ran a full-page newspaper ad with a coupon. The value was right out of the promotional book of Procter & Gamble. The value was 25 cents. The ad said you could now buy a $20,000 automobile for just 19,999.75. The promotion set sales records at the dealership. An ad for another car dealer showed all his cars hanging from a clothesline. Of course they were all white. The ad proclaimed it as the August White Sale, with a coupon below. The event was very successful. (People still notice clever.)

If you can possibly do so, use buy-back coupons. This is where the customer buys the product or service and then has to mail back the coupon to obtain her refund. It is a beautiful way to build your database. You then send out quarterly correspondence to these individuals hawking what you have to sell.

You should also check out electronic coupons. If you are a participant, as a customer's merchandise gets scanned during checkout at a grocery store, if they have purchased a competing brand, out pops your own coupon. This eliminates the cost of giving coupons to people who would have purchased your brand without the coupon. And it induces that customer to give your version of the same product a whirl. Who knows, she may become a loyal customer.

Samples

Research indicates that sampling is the best way to achieve product trial or first-time buying. Procter & Gamble has been using this approach for years. Recently other types of businesses have used sampling. Right now you can purchase a General Motors automobile, drive it for sixty days, and if you don't want to keep it, you can return the car and get all your money back. This strategy was originated by Lee Iacocca at

Chrysler years ago and everybody thought he was nuts, but few people returned the car. Today, many companies send you a sample of what they are selling for a free trial period, usually for between thirty and ninety days. In most cases, you can keep the sample even if you don't agree to sign up for their program.

Premiums

McDonald's is the king of premiums. They are constantly offering premiums that the kids love and consequently, it brings in the whole family. Be sure your premium is desirable to a member of your target audience and can't be obtained anyplace else. You may want to offer a self-liquidating premium in your ads. This is the type you offer at a very low price and where customers send money and vouchers or proof of purchase to obtain a premium gift. American Express does this all the time.

Effective premium strategies are not limited to consumer goods. A manufacturer of heavy earth-moving equipment mailed out miniature electric trains to prospective customers. In a series of mailings, the prospects received various train cars used for hauling, such as a tanker, then a caboose, and finally the engine. After the completion of the mailing, the manufacturer's sales force had little problem setting up appointments with the recipients, especially the one-third that kept the complete train set on top of their desk.

Point of Purchase (POP)

A POP display can be a very effective sales tool because it's located right next to the merchandise—but unless it's unique and stands out from the competition, it won't get you much of a bump. This is the mistake companies are making in grocery stores. Their self-talkers, the little posters attached near the merchandise, are all the same. When I worked on the Hamm's Beer account, we put together a fifteen-foot-tall end-of-aisle display featuring the Hamm's bear, who skated around on the fixture. We offered it to retailers for the weekend if they would purchase 200 cases of the beer. The demand was so great we had retailers standing in line for weeks.

If you are selling off shelves in retail stores, you want to take into account the physical challenges facing elderly shoppers. Drugstore chain Rite Aid is revising its private-label goods with bigger package fonts. Family Dollar is adapting new lighting and shelf labels. Walgreens plans to install call buttons near heavy merchandise like bottled water and laundry detergent and magnifying glasses on store shelves.

Sweepstakes and Contests

In a sweepstakes, you cannot force the participant to purchase your merchandise. That is because no skill is involved and it is thus considered a lottery, which is illegal for a for-profit company. However, you can require a purchase for a contest. Whether you choose a sweepstakes or a contest, the key question is always going to be "Who will participate?" You must structure your campaign so that your target audience is well represented among the participants.

As always, try to be unique. In 1995 Mars ran the M&M Color Campaign and collected millions of dollars in free publicity. Participants had the choice of selecting purple, blue, or pink as the color for the new variety of M&M. The announcement of the winning color—blue—was carried on most television networks. The company had the Empire State Building lighted in blue that night, resulting in wide print media coverage.

Promotions

As with all parts of your marketing plan, you want to be unique for maximum effectiveness. Burger King now has what they refer to as "Whopper Bars." They are already operative in Germany, Singapore, and Venezuela and will be opening one in Miami's South Beach and one in New York's Times Square. The stores will be more modern, but the main difference is that beer will also be on the menu.

Holiday Inn now has live bed warmers for guests. Management will send a staff member in a fleece sleeper suit to warm a guest's bed before they go to sleep. Bloomingdale's flagship store on Lexington Avenue in New York City now has what they call "Big Window Challenge." Each brand sponsors a window display that showcases a room featuring its own signature look, personality, and lifestyle. The winner was Eddie Ross, for *Elle Décor*, who presented "The Modern Woman," a room that brings together vintage and modern colors, patterns, and details. An aura of happiness, confidence, and adventure permeates the room among hot pink candlesticks, an orange art deco painting, and twin turquoise blue lamps.

Brochures

Back in Chapter 1 we told you not to put a picture of the torsion spring manufacturing facility on the cover of your sales brochure. We repeat that admonition here: When you are writing a sales brochure, remember that you are not selling the building that contains your home office; please don't put a picture of the building on the cover. As always, you lead with your benefits to get the reader to open up the brochure. I recently received a brochure from American Express. On the cover were the words, "Skyguide Executive Privilege Club." The background was a rather boring series of plane outlines. On the inside of the brochure was a list of neat benefits. That's OK if the person opens it, but this particular cover didn't give you a good reason for doing so.

Another common mistake is putting the copy on the inside of the brochure in reverse (white copy on a dark background.) Doing this reduces your readership up to 80 percent. People do not like to read reverse copy. It is too hard on the eyes.

The companies that are doing it right are direct sales retailers with their mail catalogs. Among retailers who rely on direct sales, 62 percent say their biggest revenue generator is a paper catalog. "There will be some paper version for as long as I'm in the business," says Steve Fuller, chief marketing officer for L.L. Bean.[1]

Direct Mail

The best combination for direct mail is a brochure, letter, and a postage-paid return postcard. The brochure and the letter should each tell the whole story, but in a different way. The postcard should have a couple of boxes to check. They could be "have a consultant call," "send me more material," and "not interested." Use the word consultant rather than salesperson. Include a "not interested" box because if a postcard with this box checked is returned, it probably means the participant is in fact interested in your promotion (otherwise, why would they bother responding at all?) but that you are doing something wrong in the presentation.

Try to put a benefit next to the address on the envelope. For an insurance company, I put a picture of some children on the envelope with the words, "Protect your kids."

Trade Shows

The software file TRADE.xls can be used to determine the effectiveness or value of your trade shows, brochures, coupons, or bingo cards (game cards). Ideally you would like to trace the specific type of activity relative to the number of sales consummated. Some companies can physically track a lead all the way to the eventual sale. However, many businesses, especially those marketing industrial products, cannot. They may talk to a prospect today and the sale will not be consummated for a year or two. Companies in this situation never really determine the true value of a particular trade show or brochure. They could be running trade shows or sending out brochures, using bingo cards, etc., for years and never know whether it is a losing proposition or not.

This model is based on the premise that practically all companies can trace their leads at least to the number of sales presentations that are eventually made. If you can do so, then you can place a value on each of the leads that you get from each of the preceding types of marketing communications activities and use that information to determine whether you should continue to employ a particular tactic.

Let's take a look at the case history from CTRADE, shown in Figure 10-1. The particular event is a trade show and the cost is $100,000. The number of sales presentations that have been made by the sales force during the last five years is 100,000, and the number of sales that have been made during this same period is 9,876. All companies have this type of data and based on these figures, you can determine your "closure rate." The "closure rate" is the percent of total sales presentations that are made that eventually result in a sale. For this particular company, if they have made 100,000 sales presentations over a period of years, and sales were 9,876, it means that the closure

Figure 10–1 Inquiry analysis (CTRADE).

Inquiry Analysis

Event	ASAM Trade Show	Number of Presentations (last 5 yrs.)	100,000
Product/Service	Pear	Number of Sales (last 5 years)	9,876
Date	30-Jun-06	Profit per Sale	$675
Cost	$100,000		

Week Number	Number Inquiries	Cum Inquiries	Qualified Leads	Cum. Qualified Leads	Number Sales Presentations	Cum Sales Presentations	Cost Qualified Lead	Cost Sales Presentation	Value Sales Presentation
1	25	25	15	15	6	6	$6,667	$16,667	$67
2	75	100	67	82	34	40	$1,220	$2,500	$67
3	157	257	98	180	34	74	$556	$1,351	$67
4	325	582	230	410	78	152	$244	$658	$67
5	480	1,062	305	715	98	250	$140	$400	$67
6	569	1,631	345	1,060	105	355	$94	$282	$67
7	318	1,949	213	1,273	89	444	$79	$225	$67
8	213	2,162	112	1,385	43	487	$72	$205	$67
9	89	2,251	43	1,428	21	508	$70	$197	$67
10	34	2,285	17	1,445	5	513	$69	$195	$67
11	23	2,308	12	1,457	3	516	$69	$194	$67
12	8	2,316	3	1,460	0	516	$68	$194	$67
13	3	2,319	0	1,460	0	516	$68	$194	$67
14	14	2,333	4	1,464	1	517	$68	$193	$67
15	9	2,342	2	1,466	0	517	$68	$193	$67

rate is slightly less than 10 percent. The next variable is the profit per sale. In this particular company, it's $675.00. If the profit per sale is $675.00 and the sales force closes on approximately one out of ten sales presentations, then the value of a sales presentation is $67.00. This is shown in the column to the far right in the model.

For this trade show, the number of inquiries received by the company are shown by week in the second column, with the third column being a cumulative total. The fourth column is the number that will qualify. All leads should be qualified by some means; usually the best way is through telemarketing. That means someone in your company actually calls up the person who has submitted the lead to determine whether they are a member of the target audience. The next column is a cumulative total on the number of qualified leads. Following that is the number of sales presentations made. For example, the company sent out to the sales team fifteen of the qualified leads received from week one, and of those fifteen, the sales force was able to make presentations to six of them. During the second week, eighty-two qualified leads were sent out to the field, and the sales force was able to make thirty-four sales presentations.

The seventh column from the left gives you a cumulative total of the number of sales presentations followed by the cost per qualified lead, the cost for each sales presentation, and finally, the value per sales presentation as previously discussed. You will note that at the end of week 15, the cost for each of the sales presentations was $193, while the value of a sales presentation is only $67. Obviously, it's not working for this particular company to participate in this trade show.

The cost of a sales presentation is determined by dividing the number of sales presentations that are actually made into the cost of the event, which in this particular case was $100,000. The sales force made 517 sales presentations and 517 divided into 100,000 is $193. The cost of sending the salesperson out to make the presentation is not included because the value of the sales presentation is based on the profit for selling each unit. This profit figure has already taken into account the costs of marketing.

The way to use this model is to adapt it to your various activities such as brochures, bingo cards, and trade shows, and determine which one is giving you the lowest cost on a sales presentation. Whenever you find an activity where the cost of a sales presentation is less than the value of a sales presentation, you've got yourself a winner.

Figure 10–2 depicts this particular case history as a graph. The value of a sales presentation is the horizontal line from the Y axis at $67. The cost of a qualified lead cuts below the value of a sales presentation after week 7. However, every qualified lead does not result in a sales presentation. The curve on the cost for a sales presentation gets no lower than $193, therefore, for this particular activity, the cost for each sales presentation is costing the company $193, and the value of each of these presentations is only $67. Obviously, this is a misuse of funds.

Figure 10–3 shows a copy of the inquiry analysis file from TRADE.xls where you can insert your own data. You will

Figure 10–2   Cost versus value (CTRADE; Chart).

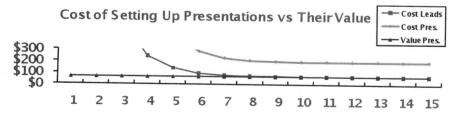

Figure 10–3 Your inquiry analysis (TRADE).

Inquiry Analysis

Event _____   # of Sales Presentations (last 5 years) _____
Product/Service _____   # of Sales (last 5 years) _____
Date _____   Profit per Sale _____
Cost _____

Week #	# Inq.	Cum. Inq.	Qual. Leads	Cum Qu. Leads	# Sls Pres.	Cum Sls Pres.	Cost Q.L.	Cost S.P.	Value Sls Pres.
1	___	0	___	0	___	0	$0	$0	$0
2	___	0	___	0	___	0	$0	$0	$0
3	___	0	___	0	___	0	$0	$0	$0
4	___	0	___	0	___	0	$0	$0	$0
5	___	0	___	0	___	0	$0	$0	$0
6	___	0	___	0	___	0	$0	$0	$0
7	___	0	___	0	___	0	$0	$0	$0
8	___	0	___	0	___	0	$0	$0	$0
9	___	0	___	0	___	0	$0	$0	$0
10	___	0	___	0	___	0	$0	$0	$0
11	___	0	___	0	___	0	$0	$0	$0
12	___	0	___	0	___	0	$0	$0	$0
13	___	0	___	0	___	0	$0	$0	$0
14	___	0	___	0	___	0	$0	$0	$0
15	___	0	___	0	___	0	$0	$0	$0

probably have to work with someone from accounting/finance to get meaningful data from a campaign your company has run. You may not be able to get the information in a usable form, but going forward, you know what you will need as per the data shown in the case history.

Objectives and Strategies

Following is a worksheet you can use to write your objectives and strategies for your entire sales promotion plan, with some suggested topics. You can substitute your own categories if these are not useful. Since you will be developing your objectives and strategies differently for each event, you will want to make as many photocopies of the worksheet (or printouts from the Worksheets folder) as you think you will need.

Be sure to make a list of your goals for *each* event or type of sales promotion identifying a specific business purpose with quantifiable objectives. "Sometimes people get so caught up in the event itself they forget what they're seeking to accomplish there," says Roger Dow, president and CEO of the U.S. Travel Association. "If you're sending people to a trade show, have them list the top five clients they want to meet and their objective for each one. When they come back, ask them what actually happened and how their meeting will benefit the organization.

Worksheet 10–1   Sales promotion plan: Objectives and strategies

Objectives

1. # of presentations and closure rate: _____

   _____

2. # Merchandise moved: _____

   _____

3. # of mailings: _____

   _____

4. # of promotions: _____

   _____

Strategies

1. _____

   _____

2. _____

   _____

3. _____

   _____

4. _____

   _____

Note

1. Jeffrey Ball, "In Digital Era, Marketers Still Prefer a Paper Trail," *Wall Street Journal*, October 16, 2009; http://online.wsj.com/article/NA_WSJ_PUB:SB125565110691488935.html.

11 · The Public Relations Plan

Public relations activity includes the following areas:

- ➢ Product/service publicity
- ➢ Charity
- ➢ Customer perceptions
- ➢ Internal marketing
- ➢ Community relations

Let's examine each of them briefly.

Product/Service Publicity

A publicity story about a company is worth how many ads? No one knows for sure, but it has to be more than one. And the price is right. In addition, the press is constantly looking for material to fill their pages on time. Approximately one-third of the articles in print publications originate outside of the press room. Therefore, someone in your business, preferably with writing skills, should be constantly looking for a publicity angle that will appeal to the press. If you are selling an iPhone or Windows 7, it may be relatively easy, but Bloomingdale's managed to obtain a half-page publicity article in the *New York Times* on the revamp of their cosmetic department.[1]

Here's a story that illustrates how powerful public relations can be: I was an account executive for an advertising agency charged with planning the introduction of Fresca into the New York City market. We were running TV commercials that showed teenagers shooting pool or doing other activities and when they started drinking Fresca, it would start to snow. The more they drank, the harder it would snow and at the end of the commercial it was a raging blizzard. The tag line was, "The frosty, freezing taste of Fresca, it's a blizzard." We scheduled an evening press party to commemorate the introduction and when I looked out my office window about two in the afternoon, I noticed it was snowing. By the time the press party started, it was like a blizzard outside.

After the press party was over, we called the *New York Times* and said we wanted to reserve space for a full-page back of section ad in the morning edition. We had to call three times because they thought we were all drunk, but on the third call they said they would reserve the space and the ad had to be there by midnight. If not, we would still have to pay for the space. We went out in the blizzard and took a picture of our CEO holding a bottle of Fresca. When New Yorkers shoveled their way to their morning newspapers and turned to our ad, they saw the picture of our CEO holding the bottle of Fresca in the raging blizzard and the headline (and only copy) said, "We Apologize."

We received free publicity on this ad in every major newspaper, from coast to coast. Although there's no doubt we got lucky on this one, it goes to show that with a little ingenuity, you can receive a lot of free advertising.

Let's see how good you are in formatting a news release. Following are the facts gathered by a reporter. See how you would organize it into a news story. Study these random facts and put a check next to the very important pieces of information and an X next to those that aren't very important and could easily be placed at the bottom of this story. Lastly put a circle next to those facts that fall between the two extremes.

_____ John Williams was promoted at Johnson College in Aberdeen, South Dakota, yesterday.

_____ The promotion was announced by college president William Smathers.

_____ Williams has been on the faculty since 1974.

_____ His new assignment is chairman of the political science department.

_____ He was formerly lieutenant governor of South Dakota for one term.

_____ He has been a professor of political science at the college since 1976, after starting as an associate professor.

_____ He and his wife, Carolyn, live in Aberdeen.

_____ They have two sons.

_____ At thirty-eight, he is the youngest department head in the school's history.

_____ The political science department has a faculty of twenty.

_____ Williams plans to make the department known throughout the country as a leading center of thought on state and local government.

_____ He was a state assemblyman for two terms prior to his election as lieutenant governor in 1970. He also taught at the University of South Dakota before running for office.

_____ He has a M.A. in political science from Yale University.

_____ He was born in Twin Brooks, South Dakota.

_____   He is the author of *Passing through the State House: A Lieutenant Governor's Diary* and *The Care and Feeding of New Laws.*

_____   Johnson College has 650 political science majors.

_____   In making the announcement, Smathers said, "John's promotion is an indication of our interest in the study of state and local government. His experience in local politics and his books and articles on the subject make him the ideal person to head our expansion in this area."

_____   Smathers estimated that the school will have over two thousand political science majors and at least a tripling of the number of course offerings in the subject within ten years.

_____   Williams will head a massive recruiting drive for students and faculty over the next several years.

_____   Williams left active participation in politics in 1974 after he and ex-Governor Patrick Terming were defeated in their bid for reelection.

OK. Let's see how you did. The ensuing news story in the next day's local newspaper would be along the following lines:

> The appointment of John Williams, former lieutenant governor of South Dakota, as head of Johnson College's department of political science was announced yesterday by William Smathers, president of the Aberdeen-based school.
>
> Williams, at 38 the youngest department head in the school's 51-year history, will spearhead a drive to make Johnson a leading center for the study of state and local government.
>
> "John's experience in local politics and his books and articles on the subject make him the ideal person to head our expansion in this area," said Smathers.
>
> He added that Williams plans to concentrate on recruiting new faculty and students over the next several years.

A professor of political science at the school since 1976, Williams was lieutenant governor of the state from 1971 to 1975.

He and running mate Governor Patrick Terming were narrowly defeated by Grover Kington and Alexander Narovansky in 1974, and he joined the Johnson faculty as an associate professor shortly after leaving office.

In his new assignment, Williams will head a faculty of 20 and oversee the political science course program for a student body of 6,000.

According to President Smathers, the department's expansion plans call for a tripling of the number of political science course offerings and an increase in the number of students majoring in the subject from 650 to more than 2,000 within the next 10 years.

A native of Twin Brooks, S.D., Williams is the author of *Passing through the State House: A Lieutenant Governor's Diary, The Care and Feeding of New Laws,* and numerous articles for academic journals.

He also served two terms as a state assemblyman and was an assistant professor of political science at the University of South Dakota before running for office.

He has a M.A. in political science from Yale University.

Williams and his wife, Carolyn, reside in Aberdeen. They have two sons.

Charity

Participating in charity drives can be an effective promotional tool for improving customer perception. You see it all the time with Wal-Mart, McDonald's, even the NFL with their pink football shoes. This strategy works both ways—it helps your company's image and it helps the charity.

Take as an example the January 2010 campaign for the Girl Scouts. As posted by Dale Buss on brandchannel.com, "The theme of the Girl Scouts most recent campaign is 'Every Cookie Has a Mission: To Help Girls Do Great Things.'" [2]

The campaign and accompanying viral YouTube video focuses on the underappreciated accomplishments—which are many—of the cookie-sales program. The video, however, eschews traditional images of Girl Scouts per se and instead delivers its message through compelling copy and graphic icons. It illustrates how cookie sales help people around the world.

Consumers, in fact, do help society by purchasing cookies from local Girl Scouts encamped around card tables outside of supermarkets and at high-school sporting events. As cookie lovers salivate over the stacked boxes of Tagalongs, Thin Mints, and Samoas, they can feel good about everything their cookie purchases help the scouts accomplish.

Girl Scouts USA, the parent organization of the thousands of local Girl Scout groups around the country, wants Americans to understand how the cookie proceeds are used to support worthy causes such as victims of floods, residents of homeless shelters, and U.S. soldiers overseas. What begins as a box of cookies sold by a young woman goes to help human beings of all ages in the most dire of circumstances.

The juxtaposition between the innocent, all-American Girl Scouts and the ugly reality of human suffering may seem like a difficult connection to make, but it is there. Big time. The cookie-focused campaign is also a precursor to an overall rebranding plan by the Girl Scouts. The rebranding campaign focuses on how scouting builds confidence and leadership skills in participating girls. Just as importantly, selling cookies allows the girls to develop business skills and financial discipline.

And you just wanted a thin mint.

Customer Perception

This actually is what public relations is all about. Keep asking what you could do to improve customer loyalty. Wal-Mart is creating friends with their stance on medical insurance. A local plumber answers his phone with the phrase, "How can I make your day?" He also sends out gift certificates for free ice cream. And there was the army general, who while talking to his troops on the front lines, asked if they needed anything. One soldier said he could really use a Snickers bar. When the general got back to his headquarters, he ordered Snickers for every soldier in the field, and had them delivered to the front lines. Afterwards, one soldier said, "I would follow that general anywhere."

Internal Marketing

Delta used to be my favorite airline. The employees were very friendly and helpful. They seemed to work together well. So it did not come as a complete surprise when I heard the employees of Delta Airlines gave their CEO a present. It was a new Boeing 757. The reason the employees gave was just that he was a nice guy. They paid the $30 million price tag by having weekly deductions taken out of their paychecks. Today, I doubt that they would buy their CEO a cigar.

The question to you is would your employees buy your CEO a cigar? If not, the work is cut out for you. Do you have an internal house organ written by the employees? Do you have goals for each employee and give rewards when they achieve them? Does management talk to each employee? Do you have gatherings where a line employee can slap a management employee on the back and ask, "How ya' doin'?"

Always remember, effective internal marketing makes external marketing so much easier.

Community Relations

A good community relations program may help you obtain favorable financing for expansion, gain favorable treatment in the form of taxes and ordinances, and attract highly qualified employees. You should give thought to corporate sponsorship of various activities such as scholarship programs, performing arts programs, local athletic teams, and environmental programs.

Two examples of extensive community relations are Kmart and Sears. Kmart has donated $70 million to charity and Sears is helping renovate the homes of low-income families. Sears also saves jobs of employees who serve in the military so when they finish deployment they return to their jobs.

Objectives and Strategies

Following is your worksheet with some suggested topics. You can photocopy this page, or print out a copy from your downloaded Worksheets folder.

Worksheet 11–1   Public relations plan: Objectives and strategies

Objectives

1. # of releases and total circulation: _____

_____

_____

2. # of internal events: _____

_____

3. # of charity contact: _____

_____

4. Increase in favorable customer perception: _____

_____

Strategies

1. _____

_____

2. _____

_____

3. _____

_____

4. _____

_____

Notes

1. Ariel Kaminer, "The Makeup Floor at Bloomingdale's Puts On a New Face," *New York Times,* October 25, 2009, page 27; http://www.nytimes.com/2009/10/25/nyregion/25critic.html?_r=1&scp=1&sq=The%20Makeup%20Floor%20at%20Bloomingdale%E2%80%99s%20Puts%20On%20a%20New%20Face&st=Search.

2. http://www.brandchannel.com/home/post/2010/01/29/Girl-Scouts-USA-Begins-Viral-Leveraging-Of-Iconic-Cookie-Sales.aspx.

12 · The Sales Plan: Pricing

In determining the price for their product/service, many companies just add up all their costs and arbitrarily add a certain amount for profit—and that becomes their selling price. The question is: Is this price giving them the maximum marginal income?

Apple, Inc. is doing very well right now financially. Of course, their iPhone is a big winner. But their Mac computer only has a 7.6 percent market share in the United States as of the second quarter of 2009, and only 3.36 percent worldwide. Dell has a 26.3 percent share and Hewlett-Packard has a 26 percent share. I believe many people would agree that the Mac has better graphics and an operating system superior to that of PCs, such as Dell and HP, which run Microsoft Windows. Then why is their market share so low? I believe it is because they are premium priced. If they dropped their price to match Dell and HP would their shares double or triple?

Conversely, Australia Chardonnay wine was a good seller here in the United States until recently. They kept dropping their price to the point that people began to think it was inferior and consequently, they started losing sales. These two tales are my way of saying that you may want to do some research to see if you have an optimum price.

The first two matrixes of the pricing model (CPRICING.xls) are shown in Figure 12-1. The first matrix establishes fixed costs. This pricing model case history is based on a proposal that includes a $10,000,000 plant (shown in Figure 12-5). In this hypothetical situation, we are depreciating the building over five years or $2,000,000 per year. Corporate fixed costs are estimated to be somewhere between $300,000 and $500,000, operational fixed costs between $8,200,000 and $9,500,000, and the cost for our own staff, which includes management and others who are not directly involved in production, at $3 million. This gives a total fixed cost estimated to be somewhere between $13,500,000 and $15,000,000 per year.

The second matrix on Figure 12-1 concerns the selection of the selling price. The variables are estimated variable costs (VC high versus VC low), selling price, and estimated sales at that price. In our example, the estimated high variable cost is $1,500 and the low variable cost $1,350. In contrast to fixed costs, variable costs vary relative to the number of units. If this company comes in at its estimated high variable cost of $1,500, that means that the cost of goods, labor, and other variable costs would be approximately $1,500 per unit. After the variables are inserted, the computer will determine the marginal income per unit as well as the total marginal income for both the high and low variable costs. What you are looking for here is the price that will give you the highest total marginal income, whether you have high or low VC. We see that the highest total marginal income ($15 million and $18 million, respectively) is generated when our sales price is $2,100.

If the item is priced at $800 per unit, estimated sales are projected at 120,000 units. However, if the company came in with its high variable cost, it would lose $700 per unit and if it

Figure 12–1   Pricing model: Establishing fixed costs and selection of selling price (CPRICING; range name: First Half).

Pricing Model   Range Name: First Half

Establishing Fixed Costs

Item	Fixed Cost (low)	Fixed Cost (high)
Deprec.	$2,000,000	$2,000,000
Corporate	$300,000	$500,000
Operations	$8,200,000	$9,500,000
Staff	$3,000,000	$3,000,000
Total FC	$13,500,000	$15,000,000

Selection of Selling Price

Selling Price Range	Est. Sales (units)	Marginal Income Per Unit High VC $1,500	Low VC $1,350	Total Marginal Income High Var. Cost	Low Var. Cost
$800	120,000	($700)	($550)	($84,000,000)	($66,000,000)
$900	100,000	($600)	($450)	($60,000,000)	($45,000,000)
$1,000	84,000	($500)	($350)	($42,000,000)	($29,400,000)
$1,300	60,000	($200)	($50)	($12,000,000)	($3,000,000)
$1,500	40,000	$0	$150	$0	$6,000,000
$1,800	34,000	$300	$450	$10,200,000	$15,300,000
$2,100	25,000	$600	$750	$15,000,000	$18,750,000
$2,500	12,000	$1,000	$1,150	$12,000,000	$13,800,000
$2,800	10,000	$1,300	$1,450	$13,000,000	$14,500,000

came in with its low variable cost, it would lose $550 per unit. At the other extreme we see the high selling price of $2,800. Here the sales projection is 10,000 units. The marginal income per unit would be $1,300 if the company comes in with its high variable cost and $1,450 if they come in with their low variable cost. However, because the total unit sales are so low (10,000), this high price still does not give us our highest total marginal income. Total marginal income is the marginal income per unit (selling price minus variable cost) times estimated sales.

As we see in Figure 12–1, at a selling price of $2,100, the total marginal income is estimated to be between $15,000,000 and $18,750,000.

Figure 12–2 (Total Marginal Income) shows a chart from the Excel file (chart name: MARGINCOM) illustrating the total marginal income for both the high and low variable costs. Notice that each line chart peaks at $2,100. Figure 12–3 (Price/Volume Relationship) is an XY chart from the Excel file (chart name: PRICEVOL) depicting the relationship between the various prices and the estimated volume for each. This line should always be a relatively smooth curve, with the curve being close to the horizontal for products or services that are insensitive to price (for example, Scotch) and more vertical when they are price sensitive (for example, paper napkins, paper towels, etc.).

Figure 12–2   Total marginal income (CPRICING; chart name: MARGINCOM).

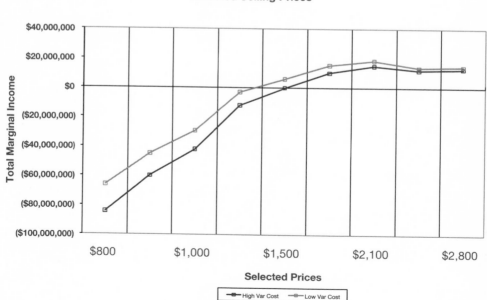

It is clear from the slope of the curve that our hypothetical product is price sensitive.

The second half of the pricing model (range name: Second Half), as shown in Figure 12–4, determines the high and low marginal income on both a unit and a percentage basis. The two variables are the high and low sales price. In the previous section of the model, it was determined that the optimum sales price should be $2,100. That figure is inserted in the column marked high in the model. For the low price we have taken the price immediately below the highest price. The reason for this is that even if you price a product or service at $2,100, the trade is going to try and beat you down to get a lower price. After we have inserted our two variables, the computer model picks up the low variable cost against a high sales price to give us our maximum marginal income per unit of $750 or 36 percent. The

Figure 12–3   Price/volume relationship (CPRICING; chart name: PRICEVOL).

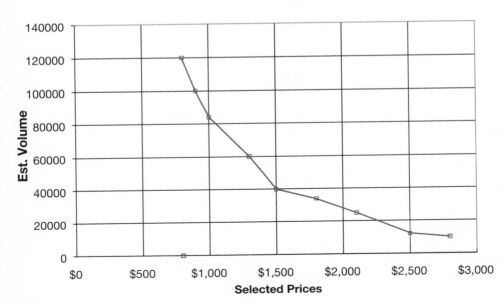

Price/Volume Relationship

other extreme or least favorable scenario would mean a $1,800 sales price with our high variable cost of $1,500, giving us a marginal income per unit of only $300, which is a mere 17 percent return.

Now that we have our high and low marginal income, we can determine our breakeven points, which is the second part of this figure. The column on the left is our most favorable scenario and the column to the far right is our least favorable scenario. For example, if we come in with our low fixed cost of

Figure 12–4   Pricing model: High/low marginal income, breakeven points, and net income (CPRICING; range name: Second Half).

Pricing Model

Range Name: Second Half

High/Low Marginal Income (Units & Percent)

Item	High	Low
Sales Price	$2,100	$1,800
Var. Cost	$1,350	$1,500
M.I./Unit	$750	$300
M.I. (%)	35.71%	16.67%

Breakeven Points

Low F.C. High M.I.	High F.C. High M.I.	Low F.C. Low M.I.	High F.C. Low M.I.
$37,800,000	$42,000,000	$81,000,000	$90,000,000

Net Income

Year	Sales Growth 5%	Sales*M.I. 26%	Less Ave. Fix. Costs	Net Income
1	$57,525,000	$15,066,071	$14,250,000	$816,071
2	$60,401,250	$15,819,375	$14,250,000	$1,569,375
3	$63,421,313	$16,610,344	$14,250,000	$2,360,344
4	$66,592,378	$17,440,861	$14,250,000	$3,190,861
5	$69,921,997	$18,312,904	$14,250,000	$4,062,904

$13,500,000 and our high marginal income of $750 per unit or 36 percent, then our breakeven point is only $37,800,000. However, if we come with our high fixed cost of $15,000,000 and our low marginal income of only $300 per unit or 17 percent, our breakeven point skyrockets all the way up to $90,000,000.

The third matrix on Figure 12–4 gives us our net income. The variables here are annual sales growth rate and first-year sales. First-year sales can either be the recommended sales price of $2,100 multiplied by estimated sales of 25,000 units, or, if you wanted to be conservative, it could be an average of the high and low selling price times the average for the estimated sales for each of these particular prices. For example, you could take the average between $2,100 and $1,800, which would be $1,950; and the average between the estimated sales for each price, 34,000 and 25,000, or 29,500. Multiplying $1,950 times 29,500 units would give you the first-year sales of $57,525,000. To determine the marginal income, the computer takes the average between the previously calculated high and low margins (36 percent and 17 percent) or 26 percent. Therefore, after subtracting the estimated average cost for labor, cost of goods, etc., marginal income for the first year will be $15,660,071. From this is subtracted average fixed cost of $14,250,000, resulting in a net income of $816,071. For years 2 through 5, the computer increases annual sales at the rate of 5 percent, which will provide an annual net income at the end of year 5 of $4,062,904.

The last part of our hypothetical pricing model, as shown in Figure 12–5, is discounted cash flow.

Actually, the most important factor or number in this entire model is a variable that you see underneath the discount factor in the far right-hand column. What the 17.4 percent means is that if all the preceding figures are correct, then you will be receiving a 17.4 percent return on your money after taxes. We'll

Figure 12–5   Discounted cash flow (CPRICING; range name: DCF).

Discounted Cash Flow

Range Name: DCF

Year	Net Income After Tax 46.00%	Add Back Deprec.	Initial Cost	Total Cash Flow	Discount Factor 17.40%
			$10,000,000	($10,000,000)	$9,053
1	$440,679	$2,000,000		$2,440,679	
2	$847,463	$2,000,000		$2,847,463	
3	$1,274,586	$2,000,000		$3,274,586	
4	$1,723,065	$2,000,000		$3,723,065	
5	$2,193,968	$2,000,000		$4,193,968	

return to this figure in a moment. Going over to the left-hand side of this part of the model, the variable is the tax rate. What has been inserted is 46 percent. The computer then multiplies the net income from the preceding part of the model, giving us a net income after taxes of $440,679 for the first year. Then adding back in depreciation, you get a total cash flow at the end of the first year of $2,440,679. The cash outlay or the cost of the plant ($10,000,000) is shown underneath the initial cost column. For years 1 through 5, the total cash flow is $16,479,760. On a discount factor or net present value, this gives you a 17.4 percent return on your money.

The net present value formula goes in the cell that currently contains $9,053. Then, after you have completed all parts of the model, you keep varying the percentage figure immediately under the column titled "discount factor" until the number two rows below becomes the closest to zero. For example, if you change the discount factor from 17.4 percent to 17.5 percent, the figure two rows below would become –16,046. If you change the discount factor to 17.3, it would become 34,251. Therefore, 17.4 percent is the correct discount factor or return on this company's money. (We used this reasoning in calculating discounted cash flow when we were discussing the product/service plan, back in Chapter 6, remember?)

Obviously, a 17.4 percent return after taxes is very favorable. If management of this hypothetical company were in agreement with all of the previous figures in this model, then quite likely the company would go ahead with this proposal because it gives a very attractive return. If the return was only 5–10 percent after taxes, then most likely it would not be a viable project. The reason is that it's possible to buy municipal bonds at a 10–12 percent return with no taxes and little risk.

Figures 12-6, 12-7, and 12-8 show the two ranges in the electronic file PRICING.xls, which you can use for your own

Figure 12–6 Your pricing model: Establishing fixed costs and selection of selling price (PRICING; range name: First Half).

Pricing Model

Range Name: First Half

Establishing   Fixed   Costs

Item	Fixed Cost (low)	Fixed Cost (high)
Deprec.	——	——
Corporate	——	——
Operations	——	——
Staff	——	——
Total FC	$0	$0

Selection of Selling Price

Selling Price Range	Est. Sales (units)	Marginal Income Per Unit High VC	Total Marginal Income Low VC	High Var. Cost	Low Var. Cost
——	——	$0	$0	$0	$0
——	——	$0	$0	$0	$0
——	——	$0	$0	$0	$0
——	——	$0	$0	$0	$0
——	——	$0	$0	$0	$0
——	——	$0	$0	$0	$0
——	——	$0	$0	$0	$0
——	——	$0	$0	$0	$0
——	——	$0	$0	$0	$0

Figure 12–7   Your pricing model: High/low marginal income, breakeven points, and net income (PRICING; range name: Second Half).

Pricing Model

Range Name: Second Half

High/Low Marginal Income (Unit & Percent)

Item	High	Low
Sales Price	____	____
Var. Cost		
M.I./Unit	$0	$0
M.I. (%)	0.00%	0.00%

Breakeven Points

	Low F.C. High M.I.	High F.C. High M.I.	Low F.C. Low M.I.	High F.C. Low M.I.
	$0	$0	$0	$0

Net Income

Year	Sales Growth	Sales*M.I. 0%	Less Ave. Fix. Costs	Net Income
1	____	$0	$0	$0
2	$0	$0	$0	$0
3	$0	$0	$0	$0
4	$0	$0	$0	$0
5	$0	$0	$0	$0

Figure 12–8   Your discounted cash flow (PRICING; range name: DCF).

Discounted Cash Flow

Range Name: DCF

Year	Net Income After Tax	Add Back Deprec.	Initial Cost	Total Cash Flow	Discount Factor
1	$0	$0	____	$0	$0
2	$0	$0		$0	
3	$0	$0		$0	
4	$0	$0		$0	
5	$0	$0		$0	

data. Remember, you only fill in the blue areas and zeros. The black zeros are formulas.

The reason the discounted cash flow factor is so helpful is that it enables you to compare the rate of return on your money for various projects or ventures. This particular project would return 17.4 percent after taxes. This can be compared with the current return on the stock market, money funds, bonds, etc., as well as various other projects. In addition to the rate of return, the other factor to be examined is risk. For example, if a company was able to obtain 10 percent return after taxes on a venture that had a very low risk such as municipal bonds, this would probably be a better investment than introducing a new product or service that only promised a 12 percent return. In this particular case, there is only a two-point spread between something that has very little risk versus a product or service introduction, which of course always involves considerable risk.

This is the first of two chapters on the Sales Plan. The objectives and strategies worksheet for this segment will be at the end of the next chapter.

13 · The Sales Plan: Future Sales

The computer files discussed in this chapter can be used for the introduction of a new product or service or an existing business to help you determine your sales forecasts, market share, and profit and loss.

In our case history file, CSALES.xls, you will see data relative to such factors as what percent of the potential buyers will become aware of what is being sold, future coverage area or distribution goals, sales closure rate, etc. By manipulating this data, you can see what effect each variable can have on the outcomes: sales, market share, profit, etc. And you will get a feel for how the model works.

If you were setting out to design this type of model, you would insert your objectives of the business at the bottom of the model and then add all the intangibles that influence these objectives at the top of the model. You would then add formulas between the intangibles and the objectives relative to how the intangibles influence the objectives.

This has already been done for you in this model. It is ready for you to insert your estimates and see what effect it has on your objectives. You can ask yourself, "What if sales closure rate increases x percent? What effect would it have on sales?" To answer this question, you insert the new closure rate and then scroll down to the objective to see the results. You keep altering your estimates until you reach the objectives you are seeking.

Then, in your marketing plan (see Worksheet 13–1 at the end of this chapter), you state how you are going to obtain the estimate you inserted for each intangible and if your marketing plan execution is successful, you should obtain the level of objectives shown in the model.

The amounts or levels you insert for the various intangibles are estimates on your part. The more research you have on this subject, the more reliable the model. But even if you don't have all this research, inserting a "best estimate" on your part should give you a better idea of where you are going than just flying by the seat of your pants.

There are two parts to the model. The case history (CSALES.xlw) presents a hypothetical situation, with numbers or values already inserted. You can change any of the estimates to see what effect it has on the objectives. As with all Excel files, the numbers in blue are modifiable estimates; the numbers in black are formulas. The case history shows three years or thirty-six months of activity, although in your own model you can insert data for just one or two years if you desire. After you are through experimenting with the case history, you can bring up your file, SALES.xlw, and insert your estimates in the cells with blue lines

This model is divided into six ranges and has ten charts.

The six matrixes are:

1. Trial transactions (range name: Trial)
2. Repeat purchases (range name: Repeat)
3. Unit and dollar volume (range name: Volume)
4. Share of market (range name: Share)

5. Profit and loss (range name: Profit)
6. Market pricing and value (range name: Pricing)

The ten charts are:

1. Awareness and distribution
2. Trial
3. New triers and total repeat
4. Costs
5. Unit market share
6. Dollar market share
7. First-year sales and profit
8. Second-year sales and profit
9. Third-year sales and profit
10. Yearly sales and profit

Let's work our way through these matrixes, starting with Trial Transactions (see Figure 13–1). This matrix calculates the number of customers who will try or buy what you are selling for the first time. It consists of nine factors (A through I) that are either your estimate or a formula.

Let's look at each of the variables involved.

A. **Total number of potential buyers** represents the total size of the market in which you operate. It would consist of your customers plus competitors' customers plus all individuals or companies that are in the market to buy what you sell but have not yet bought from either you or your competitors. This is a variable you do not control, but it is a variable because the size of a market varies from one market to the next. This number can only be an estimate, but you should acquire as much data as you can to help you in your estimate because this gives you an idea of the total po-

Figure 13–1　Trial transactions (CSALES; range name: Trial).

Trial Transactions

Range Name: Trial

A. Total Number Potential Buyers (000):　　75,000
B. Sales Closure Rate:　　28.00%

	C. Potential Buyers Aware %	D. Newly Aware (000)	E. Cum Aware (000)	F. Distribution %	G. New Trial (000)	H. Cum Trial (000)	I. Potential Buyers Trying
Month							
0	0%	0	0	10%	0	0	0
1	3%	2,250	2,250	20%	126	126	0.17%
2	6%	2,250	4,500	25%	158	284	0.38%
3	10%	3,000	7,500	29%	244	527	0.70%
4	13%	2,250	9,750	33%	208	735	0.98%
5	16%	2,250	12,000	36%	227	962	1.28%
6	19%	2,250	14,250	39%	246	1,208	1.61%
7	22%	2,250	16,500	42%	265	1,472	1.96%
8	25%	2,250	18,750	45%	284	1,756	2.34%
9	28%	2,250	21,000	48%	302	2,058	2.74%
10	31%	2,250	23,250	51%	321	2,379	3.17%
11	34%	2,250	25,500	54%	340	2,720	3.63%
12	37%	2,250	27,750	57%	359	3,079	4.10%
13	38%	750	28,500	58%	122	3,200	4.27%
14	39%	750	29,250	59%	124	3,324	4.43%
15	40%	750	30,000	60%	126	3,450	4.60%
16	41%	750	30,750	61%	128	3,578	4.77%
17	42%	750	31,500	62%	130	3,709	4.94%
18	43%	750	32,250	63%	132	3,841	5.12%
19	44%	750	33,000	64%	134	3,975	5.30%
20	45%	750	33,750	65%	137	4,112	5.48%
21	46%	750	34,500	66%	139	4,250	5.67%
22	47%	750	35,250	66%	139	4,389	5.85%
23	48%	750	36,000	66%	139	4,528	6.04%
24	49%	750	36,750	66%	139	4,666	6.22%
25	50%	750	37,500	66%	139	4,805	6.41%
26	51%	750	38,250	66%	139	4,943	6.59%
27	52%	750	39,000	66%	139	5,082	6.78%
28	53%	750	39,750	66%	139	5,221	6.96%
29	54%	750	40,500	66%	139	5,359	7.15%
30	55%	750	41,250	66%	139	5,498	7.33%
31	56%	750	42,000	66%	139	5,636	7.52%
32	57%	750	42,750	66%	139	5,775	7.70%
33	58%	750	43,500	66%	139	5,914	7.88%
34	59%	750	44,250	66%	139	6,052	8.07%
35	60%	750	45,000	66%	139	6,191	8.25%
36	61%	750	45,750	66%	139	6,329	8.44%

tential sales in your market and helps determine your market share. It does not represent the dollars; rather, it is the number of potential purchasers.

B. **Sales closure rate** represents your estimate of what percent of the potential buyers who become aware of you will try your service or buy what you have to sell for the first time. Put down the best estimate you can make and then check your number as you roll out your marketing plan.

C. **Potential buyers aware** represents your estimate of what percent of the potential buyers will become aware of your business each month after you start executing your marketing plan through the use of sales teams, advertising, sales promotion, public relations, etc.

D. **Newly aware** is a formula that gives you the number of individuals or companies that become aware of you each month. It is based on **C. Potential buyers aware** times **A. Total number of potential buyers.**

E. **Cumulative aware** is a formula and is the cumulative total of **D. Newly aware.**

F. **Distribution** is your estimate of what percent of the total potential buyers can conveniently buy from you if they so desire. If you have sales people who cover 60 percent of the territory, then you have 60 percent distribution. If you have three stores and 80 percent of the potential buyers can conveniently come to one of your stores, you have 80 percent distribution. If you sell via the Internet, then the number of clicks to your site should be added to your coverage (see Chapter 16, The Internet Plan).

G. **New trial** or first purchases is a formula consisting of **C. Potential buyers aware** times **B. Sales closure rate** times **F. Distribution.**

H. **Cumulative trial** is a formula and is the cumulative total of **G. New trial**.

I. **Potential buyers trying** is a formula of **G. New trial** divided by **A. Total number of potential buyers.**

Figure 13–2 is a chart in the Excel file that illustrates the relationship between awareness and distribution.

After you complete this range in your own matrix (SALES .xlw; see Figure 13–11), you will have an estimate of the number of new customers.

Now, let's move on to repeat purchases.

The matrix shown in Figure 13–3 calculates the number of customers that will buy your product/service more than once. It consists of eleven factors (J through T) that are either your estimate or a formula. They are:

J. **Average repeat purchase cycle** is your estimate of the amount of time that a customer is out of the market after

Figure 13–2   Awareness and distribution (CSALES; chart name: Awareness & Distribution).

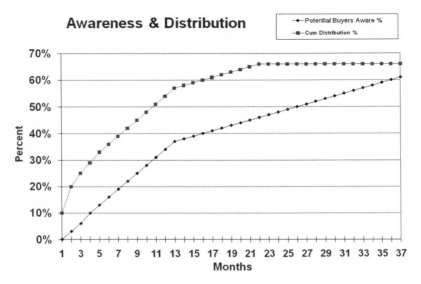

Figure 13–3   Repeat purchases (CSALES; range name: Repeat).

Repeat Purchases   Range Name: Repeat

J. Avg. Repeat Purchase Cycle (months):	2
K. Percent Triers Repeat Once (%):	40.00%
L. Percent Triers Repeat Twice (%):	60.00%
M. Percent Repeat Continuously (%):	70.00%

	N. New Triers (000)	O. First Repeat (000)	P. Second Repeat (000)	Q Cum 2nd Repeat	R Repeat Contin. (000)	S Total Repeat (000)	T Total Trans (000)	U. Repeat % Total Trans.
Month								
0	0			0		0	0	
1	126			0	0	0	126	
2	158	0		0	0	0	158	
3	244	50	0	0	0	50	294	
4	208	63	0	0	0	63	271	
5	227	97	30	30	0	128	354	
6	246	83	38	68	0	121	367	
7	265	91	58	127	21	170	435	
8	284	98	50	176	48	196	479	
9	302	106	54	231	89	249	551	
10	321	113	59	290	123	296	617	
11	340	121	64	353	162	346	686	
12	359	129	68	421	203	399	759	
13	122	136	73	494	247	456	578	
14	124	144	77	571	295	516	640	
15	126	49	82	653	346	476	602	
16	128	50	86	739	400	535	664	
17	130	50	29	768	457	537	667	
18	132	51	30	798	517	598	730	
19	134	52	30	828	538	620	754	
20	137	53	31	859	558	642	779	
21	139	54	31	890	580	665	803	
22	139	55	32	922	601	688	826	
23	139	55	32	954	623	711	849	
24	139	55	33	987	645	733	872	
25	139	55	33	1,020	668	757	895	
26	139	55	33	1,053	691	779	918	
27	139	55	33	1,087	714	803	941	
28	139	55	33	1,120	737	826	965	
29	139	55	33	1,153	761	849	988	
30	139	55	33	1,186	784	873	1,011	
31	139	55	33	1,220	807	896	1,035	
32	139	55	33	1,253	830	919	1,058	
33	139	55	33	1,286	854	942	1,081	
34	139	55	33	1,319	877	966	1,104	
35	139	55	33	1,353	900	989	1,128	
36	139	55	33	1,386	924	1,012	1,151	
Total	6,329	2,421	1,386		15,999	19,806	26,136	76%

they buy from you or a competitor. If you sell haircuts, it may be thirty days. If you sell computers, it may by two or three years.

K. **Percent triers repeat once** is your estimate of the percent of the buyers who try you or make a first purchase from you that will repeat the purchase within the time frame you inserted in J above.

L. **Percent triers repeat twice** is your estimate of the percent of buyers who repeated one purchase that you estimate will repeat a second time within the time frame you inserted in J above.

M. **Percent triers repeat continuously** is your estimate of the percent of buyers who repeated their purchase from you twice that will continue to be loyal customers.

N. **New triers** is a formula that picks up the numbers from **G. New trial** described above.

O. **First repeat** is a formula that multiplies **K. Percent triers repeat once** by **N. New triers** and deposits the number in this column one or more months later based on **J. Average repeat purchase cycle**.

P. **Second repeat** is a formula that multiplies **P. Second repeat** by **K. Percent triers repeat once** and deposits the number in this column one or more months later based on **J. Average repeat purchase cycle.**

Q. **Cumulative second repeat** is a formula that is needed to calculate **R. Repeat continuously**.

R. **Repeat continuously** is a formula that multiplies **M. Percent triers repeat continuously** by **Q. Cumulative second repeat** and deposits the number one or more months later based on **J. Average repeat purchase cycle.**

S. **Total repeats** is a formula that adds columns **O. First repeat, P. Second repeat,** and **R. Repeat continuously.**

T. **Total transactions** is a formula that adds **N. New triers** and **S. Total repeats.**

U. **Repeat % total transactions** is a formula that divides **S. Total repeats** by **T. Total transactions.**

Figure 13–4 is a graph representing New Triers and Total Repeats.

After you complete range Repeat in your own file, SALES.xlw, you will have an estimate on the total number of sales transactions (column **T**). Range Trial calculates the number of trial sales transactions and range Repeat picks up the numbers from range Trial and adds the number of repeats. The result is total sales transactions.

The next range converts transactions into unit and dollar volume.

The matrix depicted in Figure 13–5 takes the number of transactions from range Repeat and multiplies it by the esti-

Figure 13–4   New Triers and Total Repeats (CSALES; chart name: New Triers & Total Repeats).

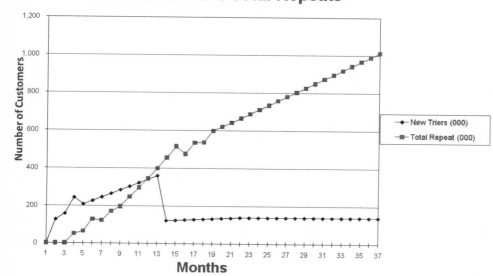

Figure 13–5 Unit and dollar volume (CSALES; range name: Volume).

Unit and Dollar Volume   Range Name: Volume

V. Average Number Units Trial Transaction: 1.10
W. Average Number Units Repeat Transaction: 1.30
X Price Per Unit: $ 0.89

Month	Y. Trial (000)	Z Repeat (000)	AA Total (000)	BB Trial (000)	CC Repeat (000)	DD Total (000)	EE Repeat % Total Dollars
		Units			Dollars		Repeat
0	0	0	0	$0	$0	$0	
1	139	0	139	$123	$0	$123	
2	173	0	173	$154	$0	$154	
3	268	66	333	$238	$58	$297	
4	229	82	311	$204	$73	$276	
5	249	166	415	$222	$148	$370	
6	270	157	428	$241	$140	$380	
7	291	221	513	$259	$197	$456	
8	312	255	566	$278	$227	$504	
9	333	323	656	$296	$288	$584	
10	353	385	738	$315	$342	$657	
11	374	450	824	$333	$400	$733	
12	395	519	914	$352	$462	$814	
13	134	593	727	$119	$528	$647	
14	136	670	807	$121	$597	$718	
15	139	619	758	$123	$551	$674	
16	141	696	837	$125	$620	$745	
17	143	697	841	$127	$621	$748	
18	146	778	923	$130	$692	$822	
19	148	806	954	$132	$717	$849	
20	150	835	985	$134	$743	$877	
21	152	864	1,017	$136	$769	$905	
22	152	894	1,046	$136	$795	$931	
23	152	924	1,076	$136	$822	$958	
24	152	954	1,106	$136	$849	$984	
25	152	984	1,136	$136	$875	$1,011	
26	152	1,013	1,166	$136	$902	$1,038	
27	152	1,044	1,196	$136	$929	$1,064	
28	152	1,074	1,226	$136	$956	$1,091	
29	152	1,104	1,257	$136	$983	$1,118	
30	152	1,134	1,287	$136	$1,010	$1,145	
31	152	1,165	1,317	$136	$1,037	$1,172	
32	152	1,195	1,347	$136	$1,064	$1,199	
33	152	1,225	1,378	$136	$1,090	$1,226	
34	152	1,255	1,408	$136	$1,117	$1,253	
35	152	1,286	1,438	$136	$1,144	$1,280	
36	152	1,316	1,468	$136	$1,171	$1,307	
Total	6,962	25,748	32,711	$6,196	$22,916	$29,112	79%

mated average number of products/services or items purchased for each sale to arrive at the unit volume. After the unit volume is calculated, this number is multiplied by the estimated dollar value per sale to arrive at total dollar volume.

This range consists of ten factors that are either your estimate or a formula (V through EE). They are:

V. **Average number units trial transaction** is an estimate of the average number of items a new customer will purchase at one time.

W. **Average number units repeat transaction** is an estimate of the average number of items a repeat customer will purchase at one time. This may be the same as V. above or you may believe a repeat customer will purchase more units because he/she is now more familiar with your product/service.

X. **Price per unit** is the selling price per unit or item.

Y. **Units trial** is a formula that multiplies **N. New triers** by **V. Average number units trial transaction** to arrive at volume in units for new customers.

Z. **Units repeat** is a formula that multiplies **S. Total repeats** by **W. Average number units repeat transaction** to arrive at volume in units for repeat customers.

AA. **Total units** is a formula that adds **Y. Units trial** and **Z. Units repeat** to arrive at total volume in units.

BB. **Dollars trial** is a formula that multiplies **Y. Units trial** by **X. Price per unit** to arrive at dollar sales from new customers.

CC. **Dollar repeat** is a formula that multiplies **Z. Units repeat** by **X. Price per unit** to arrive at dollar sales from repeat customers.

DD. **Dollars total** is a formula that adds **BB. Dollars trial** and **CC. Dollars repeat** to arrive at total dollar sales.

EE. **Repeat percent of total dollars** is a formula that divides **CC. Dollars repeat** by **DD. Total dollars.**

After you complete this range in SALES.xlw, you have your estimate on total unit and dollar volume. Isn't this a better way to arrive at your sales goals than just estimating a 5 to 10 percent increase for next year? Once sales goals have been established, the next range, range Share (see Figure 13–6), calculates share of market.

Range Share takes the unit and dollar volume estimates from range Volume and calculates share of market. Share of market is perhaps only an estimate, but it's an important factor. If you are not watching your share, you could be increasing your sales but a competitor could be increasing their sales faster and be gaining share on you. That competitor(s) could then eventually become so big that you could no longer compete with them.

Range Share consists of five factors (FF through JJ) that are either your estimate or a formula. They are:

FF. **Average market selling price** is an estimate of the price per unit. It could be the same as **X. Price per unit** unless you sell to middlemen or the trade. Even so, you want to use the price to the end user to calculate share.

GG. **Total market in units** is an estimate of the total market size in units. This would consist of your sales plus all competitor sales plus all other potential customers for the product/service you and your competitors sell.

HH. **Total market in dollars** is an estimate of the total size of the market as **GG. Total market in units**, but now you are dealing in dollars.

Figure 13-6   Share of market (CSALES; range name: Share).

Share of Market

	Range Name: Share
FF. Average Market Selling Price:	$ 1.39
GG. Total Market in Units (000):	30,000
HH. Total Market in Dollars (000):	$40,000

Month	II. Unit Share Market	JJ. Dollar Share Market
0	0.00%	0.00%
1	0.46%	0.48%
2	0.58%	0.60%
3	1.11%	1.16%
4	1.04%	1.08%
5	1.38%	1.44%
6	1.43%	1.49%
7	1.71%	1.78%
8	1.89%	1.97%
9	2.19%	2.28%
10	2.46%	2.56%
11	2.75%	2.86%
12	3.05%	3.18%
13	2.42%	2.53%
14	2.69%	2.80%
15	2.53%	2.63%
16	2.79%	2.91%
17	2.80%	2.92%
18	3.08%	3.21%
19	3.18%	3.31%
20	3.28%	3.42%
21	3.39%	3.53%
22	3.49%	3.64%
23	3.59%	3.74%
24	3.69%	3.84%
25	3.79%	3.95%
26	3.89%	4.05%
27	3.99%	4.16%
28	4.09%	4.26%
29	4.19%	4.37%
30	4.29%	4.47%
31	4.39%	4.58%
32	4.49%	4.68%
33	4.59%	4.79%
34	4.69%	4.89%
35	4.79%	5.00%
36	4.89%	5.10%

II.   **Unit share of market** is a formula that calculates unit market share and is arrived at by dividing **AA. Total units** (unit sales) by **GG. Total market in units.**

JJ.   **Dollar share of market** is a formula that calculates the dollar market share and is arrived at by multiplying **AA. Total units** times **FF. Average selling price** and dividing the total by **HH. Total market in Dollars.**

Figure 13–7 represents **JJ. Dollar share of market** as a graph. Guess this company has been doing something right.

Now that we have the estimated share of market in units and dollars, we will go on to the next to last range in the model, range Profit, to calculate a profit and loss statement (see Figure 13-8).

Range Profit uses the dollar sales from **DD. Total dollars** in range Volume along with costs to calculate profit and loss.

Figure 13–7   Dollar share of market (CSALES; chart name: Dollar Market Share).

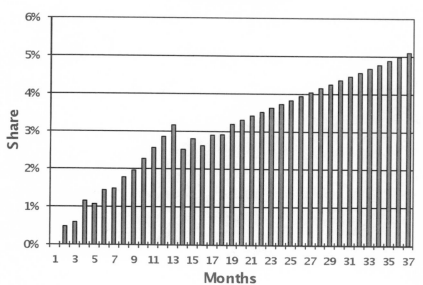

Dollar Share Market

Figure 13–8   Profit and loss (CSALES; range name: Profit).

Profit and Loss ($000)

Range Name: Profit

	KK.	LL.	MM.	NN.	OO.	PP.	QQ.
		Gross					Before Tax
First Year:	Sales	Margin	Marketing	Admin.	R&D	Deprec.	Profit
1st Q	$574	33%	$600	$110	$250	$100	($870)
2nd Q	$1,027	33%	$110	$110	$500	$100	($481)
3rd Q	$1,544	33%	$115	$125	$350	$100	($180)
4th Q	$2,204	33%	$100	$125	$200	$100	$202
Total 1st Year	$5,349		$925	$470	$1,300	$400	($1,330)
Second Year:	Sales						Profit
1st Q	$2,039	35%	$300	$125	$75	$100	$114
2nd Q	$2,315	35%	$250	$130	$75	$100	$255
3rd Q	$2,630	35%	$200	$130	$130	$100	$361
4th Q	$2,873	35%	$250	$145	$145	$100	$366
Total 2nd Year	$9,857		$1,000	$530	$425	$400	$1,095
Third Year:	Sales						Profit
1st Q	$3,113	43%	$500	$150	$110	$100	$479
2nd Q	$3,355	43%	$250	$150	$110	$100	$833
3rd Q	$3,598	43%	$200	$155	$75	$100	$1,017
4th Q	$3,840	43%	$300	$155	$75	$100	$1,021
Total 3rd Year	$13,906		$1,250	$610	$370	$400	$3,350
Total 3 Years	$29,112		$3,175	$1,610	$2,095	$1,200	$3,115

This range consists of seven factors (KK through QQ) that are either estimates or a formula. They are:

KK.   **Sales** is a formula that picks up the sales figures from **DD. Total dollars.**

LL.   **Gross margin** is an estimate of what percent of total sales dollars remain after cost of goods is subtracted.

MM. **Marketing** reflects estimated marketing costs, which consists of sales, advertising, sales promotion, public relations, customer service, and market research.

NN. **Administration** reflects estimated operating costs such as accounting, telephones, rent, office supplies, employer social security payments, receptionist, taxes, insurance, etc.

OO. **Other costs** could represent R&D, depreciation, bad debts, interest, etc.

PP. **Other costs** represent a second entry spot for other costs. (If you need a third column for other costs in your file, SALES.xlw, you can add it, but be sure to move the formula in QQ. to its new spot, and incorporate the new category of other costs.)

QQ. **Profit before taxes** is a formula that picks up **KK. Sales** and multiplies it by **LL. Gross Margin** and then subtracts costs such as **MM. Marketing, NN. Administration, OO. Other costs**, and **PP. Other costs.** The result is profit before taxes.

Figure 13–9 is a bar graph of the expenses over a three-year period that we saw in Figure 13–8. You can see that some remain relatively constant, and others (R&D and marketing) are quite variable.

The last matrix in the sales module is on pricing. Figure 13–10 shows some prices and perceived values of SBU's product and the products of various competitors, as rated by prospective customers.

If you look at the chart at the bottom of Figure 13–10 you'll see that we've bisected the field with a diagonal line. You always want your price to be *below* the diagonal. In other words, you want the perceived value of your product or service to be higher than the actual price. The reason that the Toyota Camry is such a hot seller is that people think its perceived value is greater than its actual cost. Imported beer costs more than domestic, but it sells because the buyer believes its taste is far su-

Figure 13–9   Business costs (CSALES; chart name: Costs).

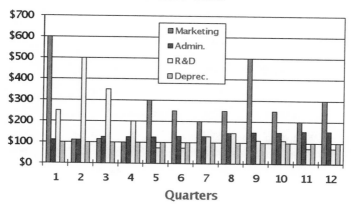

Figure 13–10   Market pricing and value (CSALES; range name: Pricing).

Market Pricing and Value

Range Name: Pricing

SBU	Perceived Value	Market Price
Company	$475	$450
Comp 1	$400	$400
Comp 2	$325	$350
Comp 3	$310	$300
Comp 4		
Comp 5		

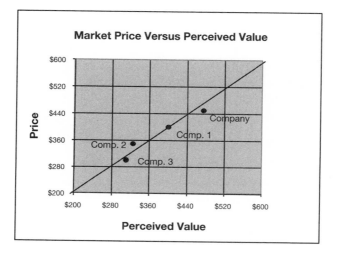

perior to a domestic beer such as Budweiser. That is the ideal situation—that your perceived value is greater than your price.

New Products/Services

When you launch a new product or service, there are some important things to keep in mind at all times. Some of them may be represented in the software (monitoring of your goals, for example), but most of them are a function of your own internal marketing and team-building skills. Note I say "internal." If you don't have everyone aware, on-board, even enthusiastic, your product launch will suffer. In particular, the goals of the launch must be known by all—and "all" means employees from all aspects of marketing: sales, marketing, customer service (yes, customer service, as we explain in Chapter 14), even accounting and finance.

Figure 13-11 is a facsimile of your first matrix for sales forecasting. Insert your estimates into the downloaded file (SALES.xlw; range name: Trial) and then take a look at your resulting objectives such as sales, profit, etc. If you don't see what you like, keep inserting different estimates until you get the objectives you want. Remember, however, you have to be able to achieve the estimates that you insert.

I believe the sales closure rate is the most important measurement in your sales plan so I am including a checklist of pointers for increasing your closure rate. You may want to share this with all your sales presenters.

Remember, sales is a part of marketing.

- ➤ Have a good ten-second opener.
- ➤ Emphasize what the product or service will do for the customer.
- ➤ Cover all important selling points on every call.

Figure 13-11   Your trial transactions (SALES; range name: Trial).

Trial Transactions

Range Name: Trial

A. Total Number Potential Buyers (000): _____

B. Sales Closure Rate: _____

Month	C. Potential Buyers Aware %	D. Newly Aware (000)	E. Cum Aware (000)	F. Distribution %	G. New Trial (000)	H. Cum Trial (000)	I. Potential Buyers Trying
0	____	0	0	____	0	0	0
1	____	0	0	____	0	0	0.00%
2	____	0	0	____	0	0	0.00%
3	____	0	0	____	0	0	0.00%
4	____	0	0	____	0	0	0.00%
5	____	0	0	____	0	0	0.00%
6	____	0	0	____	0	0	0.00%
7	____	0	0	____	0	0	0.00%
8	____	0	0	____	0	0	0.00%
9	____	0	0	____	0	0	0.00%
10	____	0	0	____	0	0	0.00%
11	____	0	0	____	0	0	0.00%
12	____	0	0	____	0	0	0.00%
13	____	0	0	____	0	0	0.00%
14	____	0	0	____	0	0	0.00%
15	____	0	0	____	0	0	0.00%
16	____	0	0	____	0	0	0.00%
17	____	0	0	____	0	0	0.00%
18	____	0	0	____	0	0	0.00%
19	____	0	0	____	0	0	0.00%
20	____	0	0	____	0	0	0.00%
21	____	0	0	____	0	0	0.00%
22	____	0	0	____	0	0	0.00%
23	____	0	0	____	0	0	0.00%
24	____	0	0	____	0	0	0.00%
25	____	0	0	____	0	0	0.00%
26	____	0	0	____	0	0	0.00%
27	____	0	0	____	0	0	0.00%
28	____	0	0	____	0	0	0.00%
29	____	0	0	____	0	0	0.00%
30	____	0	0	____	0	0	0.00%
31	____	0	0	____	0	0	0.00%
32	____	0	0	____	0	0	0.00%
33	____	0	0	____	0	0	0.00%
34	____	0	0	____	0	0	0.00%
35	____	0	0	____	0	0	0.00%
36	____	0	0	____	0	0	0.00%

- Proceed logically from one point to another.
- Anticipate objections and include answers to them in your presentation.
- Use visuals to make a point.
- Get the customer into the act.
- Say "you," not "we."
- Check your progress selling each benefit by asking questions.
- Arouse curiosity.
- How you handle your product, visual, or sales tool is as important as what you say. Be sure to handle them with respect.
- Use a sixty-second close.
- Ask for the order.

When I was a young boy I sold magazines door to door. I would ask the person who opened the door whether they would like a copy of *Colliers, Companion,* or *American*. I was not very successful. Then my father, who was in sales training, changed my opener and told me to bring my dog with me. This was in Minnesota, where it always snows. My new opener, while standing on the door step, with snow coming down and my dog by my side, was, "Would you like an evening's enjoyment?" (Remember, this was long before Netflix, or even a TV in every home.) I soon became one of the most successful magazine carriers in the state.

So many companies keep talking about the features of their product or service. If I were selling computers, I would not just stand there next to the prospect while she glanced at the various models. I would have the machines operable and ask the prospect to bring up Word and type herself a message and go to the spreadsheet and type in some numbers. You want to get the person directly involved with what you are selling, and then segue into more technical material.

If you anticipate some objections, like premium pricing, bring the factor up before your prospect does. For example, with Apple's computers, you will have fewer viruses than with a PC, so you won't lose your stuff, and better graphics that will make your presentations the best in the office. If you board dogs and are premium priced, tell the prospect that his dog will not miss him as much because he will enjoy being in a bigger cage and will have the fun of playing with other dogs several times a day.

When you are at the end of your presentation, you don't want the prospect to say I will think about it. Get her into the act. On your close, always give her a choice of two or more options. Which model, A or B, do you believe will give you the greatest increase in your office productivity? Or which deductable, $500 or $1,000, fits in best with your economic projections?

Objectives and Strategies

Following is a worksheet for your sales plan with some suggested topics. You can photocopy this or print out a copy from your downloaded Worksheets folder.

Worksheet 13–1   Sales Plan: Objectives and strategies

Objectives

1. Sales call closure rate: _____

_____

2. Trial rate: _____

_____

3. Repeat sales rate: _____
    _____

4. Distribution rate: _____
    _____

Strategies

1. _____
    _____

2. _____
    _____

3. _____
    _____

4. _____
    _____

14 · The Customer Service Plan

Customer service is not a department, it's an attitude. It has to be a part of marketing, because these employees must know all about the products and services, the advertising, public relations, and sales promotion. That is the only way they can give intelligent answers to questions by customers. They should also be aware of the company's vision, which should translate into a Disneyland mode of operation for customer service, whose reps are referred to as "my Disney team" and whose employees *all* tout Disneyland as the place "where dreams come true." Hard to imagine a more positive attitude than that.

Customer service can be a profit point as well, because research has indicated that keeping a customer only costs one-fifth as much as acquiring a new one. For example, a clerk at Nordstrom's gave a refund to a customer for returning a tire, even though Nordstrom's doesn't sell tires, and an employee at Midwest Express lent one of his business suits to a passenger who had lost his luggage. Do you think these two customers will keep coming back?

One of the most important things you can do is review all your customer service policies. Most likely they are written for

197

the benefit of the company. That's all wrong. They should be written for the benefit of the customer. What do you think when an employee says to you, "Sorry, but that is our policy"? Do you plan on going back to that store or business? Now, what if the employee said, "Sorry, that is our normal policy, but let's see if there is a way to solve your need"? All the difference in the world. Therefore, you have to talk to management about changing company policies or at least give customer service some freedom in their interpretation—all in the service of better branding and marketing.

It's also important to make it easy for the customer to complain or obtain information. How do you feel when you dial a business and you sit on the phone while the company's computer goes through about twenty extension possibilities that don't interest you? Why don't you hire a person to answer the phone on the first ring and say as the local plumber does, "How can I make your day"?

If your company discourages returns, you may be losing sales—and perhaps even customers. That's because when customers know they can return anything they buy, no questions asked, they are likely to buy more than shoppers who are afraid they may get stuck with the merchandise. According to J. Andrew Petersen and V. Kumar, there is an optimum rate of return. Higher returns, up to a point, have been shown to result in higher future sales. But if the rate of returns is too high, the cost to the company increases. You should analyze the cost of returns to your company and the effect of the returns on sales to determine what rate of return gives you the highest profit. These authors go on to suggest ways a company might discourage returns if the rate is too high.[1]

You also want to monitor service internally to be sure that employees treat each other like customers. If an employee is in a bad mood when a customer approaches, that mood will probably be perceived by the customer. Listen to everyone in the distribution chain as well. The more you know about what everyone is thinking, the more efficient customer service becomes.

Stay in touch after the sale, but not by sending out a questionnaire for the buyer to fill out. Who has the time? And besides, these satisfaction surveys are relatively meaningless, because customers don't necessarily tell the truth—I don't, do you?—and the surveys themselves are structured in a way guaranteed to avoid meaningful information: "on a scale of 1 to 5, how satisfied are you with . . ." Besides, this strategy just benefits the company. Instead, call up your customers and ask them how you can serve them better. I know a CEO that does this and usually she has to repeat herself several times because the listener doesn't think she means it. She keeps repeating herself and often the listener finally says, "Nobody has ever asked me that before." She has an outstanding repeat business.

Companies are adding "services" to their manufacturing lines. Many keep their service offerings separate from the rest of the operation, in order to ensure a sharp focus on the new and innovative service packages being sold. Truck manufacturers, for example, now may offer driver training options, or logistics management services, or even "greener trucking" programs. The more successful firms offer a generic service package, instead of the more usual "parts replacement and servicing." For instance, one truck manufacturer offers a maintenance and repair package with standardized prices for spare parts and scheduling for service (no surprises there)—but if a customer wants to use another company's replacement part, the company customizes the plan by dropping the replacement-parts feature.[2] That truck manufacturer is clearly looking out for its customers' interests—and you can bet *that* client is there for the long haul.

Objectives and Strategies

The worksheet below offers you the opportunity to develop your objective and strategies relating to customer service. You can photocopy this, or print out a copy from the Worksheets folder you downloaded to your computer. I've made suggestions as to the kinds of things you may want to address as objectives, but you should modify this worksheet to meet the needs of your company, product, or service.

Worksheet 14–1   Customer service plan: Objectives and strategies

Objectives

1. Answering time: _____

_____

2. Policies: _____

_____

3. Personality: _____

_____

4. Company and trade knowledge: _____

_____

Strategies

1. _____

_____

2. _____

_____

3. _____

_____

4. _____

_____

Notes

1. J. Andrew Petersen and V. Kumar, "Get smart about product returns," *Wall Street Journal,* November 30, 2009; http://online.wsj.com/article/SB10001424052970203585004574392464143500106.html.

2. Stephen W. Brown, Anders Gustafsson, and Lars Witell, "Beyond products," *Wall Street Journal,* June 22, 2009; http://online.wsj.com/article/SB10001424052970204830304574131273123644620.html.

15 · Maximizing High-Potential Accounts

The primary purpose of this chapter is to illustrate two common mistakes in sales development. They are:

1. Selling for volume rather than for profit.
2. Directing equal marketing pressure at all possible customers rather than concentrating on those with the highest potential.

To illustrate what I mean by this, I have put together four separate sales plans for the hypothetical Swing Corporation.

The Swing Corporation manufactures and markets an audio package for the elaborate-packaging market. Three models are offered: circuits, tubes, and valves. The sales plans are for the Northeast region, which represents approximately 10 percent of the corporation's national market. The four sales plans are titled:

1. Forecasting by Sales Volume by Customer
2. Forecasting by Net Profit by Customer

3. Forecasting by Net Profit by Customer by Product/Service
4. Forecasting by Maximizing High-Potential Accounts

Forecasting by sales volume (Plan 1) is still the most preva-
lent means of determining sales for the following year. However, the problem is that sales volume by itself is meaningless.
What good is it if you sell a million units and lose on each one?
Forecasting by net profit by customer (Plan 2) is superior to
Plan 1, but if you're selling more than one product or service to
the customer, you don't know which ones are the winners and
which ones are the losers. Therefore, forecasting by net profit
by customer by product/service (Plan 3) is more effective
than either Plan 1 or Plan 2. As you will see later in this chapter, when Plan 3 was used, it was determined that one of the
three models (valves) was a money loser.

Forecasting by maximizing high-potential accounts (Plan 4)
is based on the premise that you need to spend no more time or
money on obtaining a 30 percent share of a 100-unit potential
customer, which equates to 30 units, than on obtaining a 30 percent share of a 10-unit potential customer, which equates to only
3 units. Consequently, *marketing efforts should be concentrated
on those customers with the highest potential.* Applying this principle to the hypothetical case history, total sales are decreased 8
percent, but net profit increases 273 percent.

Forecasting by Sales Volume by Customer (Sales Plan 1)

Figure 15–1 illustrates forecasting by sales volume by customer. Column 1 contains the names of the customers. Column
2 is an estimate of the client's total purchases, from all suppliers, in the market segments in which the company competes.
The third column shows the company's sales to each of its

clients. The data from columns 2 and 3 permit you to calculate your share of market by customer. For example, it is estimated that AT&T will buy $332,678 worth of elaborate-packaging products, and Swing Corporation's share of those total purchases is estimated at $89,007, or 27 percent. The advantage of estimating your current share of market by client or account is that it permits you to forecast on the basis of share rather than sales. As mentioned, you can increase your sales and at the same time lose share. This situation could become a severe problem for you in the years ahead.

The fifth column in Figure 15–1 is an estimate of the growth in total purchases by customer for the next year. This growth rate can be applied to the current year client volume to obtain estimated client volume for the new year. Forecasting should then be based on your strategic choice of share increase, share maintenance, or share decrease. For example, the current estimated share for AT&T is 27 percent, and Swing wants to increase that share to 30 percent for the next year. Multiplying the estimated share by estimated client volume would then give you your sales forecast for the new period. In this case it's $119,764.

The next column contains the name of the salesperson as well as his or her estimate on the number of sales calls that will be needed for the new year. This information can then be used to calculate the estimated sales volume by sales call. For example, Holston estimates that he will need twenty sales calls on AT&T for the new year, and the sales forecast is $119,764. This equates to a sales volume of $5,988 for each of the twenty sales calls.

At the bottom of Figure 15–1 is a summary of the estimated sales activity for each of the five salespeople for the new year. You will notice that, given these data, Summers, if he hits his forecast, will be the most effective salesperson. His total sales

(text continues on page 208)

Figure 15-1 Forecasting by volume by customer—Plan 1.

	Current Year						Current Year + 1			
Client Name	Client Vol.	Our Sales	Share	Growth	Est. Clt. Vol.	Est. Share	Sales	Slspers.	Nb. of Calls	Sales/Call
AT&T	$332,678	$89,007	27%	20%	$399,214	30%	$119,764	Holston	20	$5,988
Amdahl	$906,783	$102,333	11%	30%	$1,178,818	12%	$141,458	Holston	30	$4,715
Apple	$1,267,490	$367,890	29%	15%	$1,457,614	30%	$437,284	Carlson	80	$5,466
Bocuzzi	$21,234	$10,890	51%	40%	$29,728	55%	$16,350	Lewis	10	$1,635
Bush	$899,067	$112,339	12%	5%	$944,020	15%	$141,603	Summers	40	$3,540
Commodore	$890,006	$113,335	13%	-20%	$712,005	15%	$106,801	Abbott	30	$3,560
Eagle	$667,889	$113,324	17%	-30%	$467,522	20%	$93,504	Abbott	30	$3,117
Farraro	$223,445	$45,667	20%	15%	$256,962	25%	$64,240	Summers	20	$3,212
Gaire	$220,890	$12,443	6%	10%	$242,979	10%	$24,298	Lewis	20	$1,215
Graft	$64,566	$43,990	68%	40%	$90,392	70%	$63,275	Carlson	20	$3,164
Green	$2,334,567	$733,324	31%	10%	$2,568,024	35%	$898,808	Abbott	50	$17,976
Hewitt	$267,590	$123,345	46%	5%	$280,970	50%	$140,485	Carlson	30	$4,683
Honeywell	$890,000	$223,445	25%	0%	$890,000	25%	$222,500	Lewis	40	$5,563
IBM	$334,689	$123,445	37%	10%	$368,158	40%	$147,263	Abbott	50	$2,945
Johnson	$3,890,563	$389,445	10%	-10%	$3,501,507	15%	$525,226	Summers	100	$5,252
Luther	$2,134,889	$256,779	12%	30%	$2,775,356	15%	$416,303	Holston	70	$5,947
Orange	$1,123,567	$222,456	20%	10%	$1,235,924	20%	$247,185	Lewis	20	$12,359
Osborne	$453,990	$111,334	25%	-15%	$385,892	25%	$96,473	Abbott	30	$3,216
Pear	$890,766	$332,456	37%	30%	$1,157,996	40%	$463,198	Lewis	40	$11,580
Peters	$111,345	$25,556	23%	20%	$133,614	25%	$33,404	Lewis	10	$3,340
Peterson	$168,766	$89,006	53%	0%	$168,766	55%	$92,821	Summers	10	$9,282
Reagan	$334,554	$231,224	69%	10%	$368,009	70%	$257,607	Holston	40	$6,440
Robin	$889,766	$289,006	32%	25%	$1,112,208	35%	$389,273	Carlson	80	$4,866
Smith	$1,222,334	$300,443	25%	15%	$1,405,684	25%	$351,421	Summers	70	$5,020
Sparrow	$162,678	$89,008	55%	10%	$178,946	55%	$98,420	Carlson	20	$4,921
Sperry	$345,213	$50,890	15%	25%	$431,516	20%	$86,303	Holston	50	$1,726

| | Current Year | | | Current Year + 1 | | | | | | |
Client Name	Client Vol.	Our Sales	Share	Growth	Est. Clt. Vol.	Est. Share	Sales	Slspers.	Nb. of Calls	Sales/Call
Stemper	$998,767	$367,889	37%	-10%	$898,890	40%	$359,556	Summers	30	$11,985
Taylor	$667,778	$111,890	17%	10%	$734,556	20%	$146,911	Holston	30	$4,897
Wang	$347,294	$134,890	39%	20%	$416,753	40%	$166,701	Abbott	60	$2,778
Washington	$324,554	$113,448	35%	20%	$389,465	40%	$155,786	Lewis	40	$3,895
Weber	$107,888	$66,554	62%	-30%	$75,522	65%	$49,089	Carlson	20	$2,454
Total	$23,495,606	$5,397,051	23%	7%	$25,257,006	26%	$6,553,311		1,190	$5,507

Current Year + 1

	Salesperson Abbott	Salesperson Carlson	Salesperson Holston	Salesperson Lewis	Salesperson Summers
Total Sales	$1,509,551	$1,177,825	$1,168,347	$1,162,721	$1,534,868
Number of Clients	6	6	6	7	6
Largest Client	$898,808	$437,284	$416,303	$463,198	$525,226
Avg. Sls. per Call per Client	$5,599	$4,259	$4,952	$5,655	$6,382
Total Nb. of Calls	250	250	240	180	270

are projected at $1,534,868, and average sales per call are expected to be $6,382.

However, this type of analysis can be very misleading if your company sells products/services with different margins. In these cases, the people who sell the most normally are not the ones who contribute the largest amount to profit. Why? Because they are selling the products/services that are the easiest to sell—and those usually have the lowest margins. Therefore, if these companies are rewarding their salespeople on the basis of volume, most likely they are rewarding the wrong people. Sales Plan 2 illustrates this fact.

Forecasting by Net Profit by Customer (Plan 2)

Sales Plan 2 is illustrated in three figures: Figure 15–2, which shows the estimated sales by product category; Figure 15–3, which calculates the margins by category and gross profit; and Figure 15–3a, which looks at expenses and profit per client per sales call.

If you are selling more than one product/service and they offer different margins, then the first step in forecasting net profit is to break out estimated sales for each. For example, we know from Sales Plan 1 (Figure 15–1) that total estimated purchases by AT&T are $119,764. In Figure 15–2, total estimated purchases are subdivided by model. It is estimated that AT&T will purchase $25,778 of the circuit model, $6,457 of the tubes model, and $87,529 of the valves model. Figure 15–2 also shows the percentage of client purchases by model type. Twenty-two percent of AT&T purchases will be for circuits, 5 percent for tubes, and 73 percent for valves. These percentage figures will be used later in Sales Plan 4 to determine company development.

In Figure 15–3, the first column contains the name of the client and columns two, three, and four list the gross profit by

Figure 15–2 Sales by product category—Plan 2.

	Estimated Sales			Percentage of Sales		
Client	Circuits	Tubes	Valves	Circuits	Tubes	Valves
AT&T	$25,778	$6,457	$87,529	22%	5%	73%
Amdahl	$31,667	$34,665	$75,126	22%	25%	53%
Apple	$122,388	$45,778	$269,118	28%	10%	62%
Bocuzzi	$3,489	$2,377	$10,484	21%	15%	64%
Bush	$54,990	$42,009	$44,604	39%	30%	31%
Commodore	$21,778	$21,990	$63,033	20%	21%	59%
Eagle	$23,556	$10,880	$59,068	25%	12%	63%
Farraro	$10,445	$23,998	$29,797	16%	37%	46%
Gaire	$16,778	$3,778	$3,742	69%	16%	15%
Graft	$12,889	$10,008	$40,378	20%	16%	64%
Green	$156,897	$245,889	$496,022	17%	27%	55%
Hewlitt	$23,990	$41,990	$74,505	17%	30%	53%
Honeywell	$128,890	$89,990	$3,620	58%	40%	2%
IBM	$12,996	$32,990	$101,277	9%	22%	69%
Johnson	$123,776	$213,887	$187,563	24%	41%	36%
Luther	$222,886	$114,667	$78,750	54%	28%	19%
Orange	$45,332	$21,996	$179,857	18%	9%	73%
Osborne	$38,776	$12,885	$44,812	40%	13%	46%
Pear	$135,665	$167,889	$159,644	29%	36%	34%
Peters	$6,775	$2,345	$24,284	20%	7%	73%
Peterson	$12,332	$21,887	$58,602	13%	24%	63%
Reagan	$49,867	$21,665	$186,075	19%	8%	72%
Robin	$56,779	$23,996	$308,498	15%	6%	79%
Smith	$23,997	$35,442	$291,982	7%	10%	83%
Sparrow	$21,886	$34,221	$42,313	22%	35%	43%
Sperry	$21,331	$14,335	$50,637	25%	17%	59%
Stemper	$47,884	$27,885	$283,787	13%	8%	79%
Taylor	$32,997	$41,885	$72,029	22%	29%	49%
Wang	$31,552	$21,998	$113,151	19%	13%	68%
Washington	$21,553	$45,331	$88,902	14%	29%	57%
Weber	$12,332	$6,755	$30,002	25%	14%	61%
Total	$1,552,251	$1,441,868	$3,559,192	24%	22%	54%

model. The margins are at the top of the column: circuits have a 17.07 percent margin; tubes, 10.59 percent; and valves, 4.15 percent. These margins are from the previous year. The fifth column contains the sum of columns two, three, and four, or total gross profit.

Moving on to Figure 15–3a, we see that the first three columns allocate the expenses per client. The first of these ex-

Figure 15–3   Margin and gross profit—Plan 2.

Client	Margins 17.07% GP Circuits	10.59% GP Tubes	4.15% GP Valves	Total GP
AT&T	$4,399	$684	$3,632	$8,715
Amdahl	$5,404	$3,671	$3,118	$12,193
Apple	$20,886	$4,848	$11,168	$36,902
Bocuzzi	$595	$252	$435	$1,282
Bush	$9,384	$4,449	$1,851	$15,684
Commodore	$3,716	$2,329	$2,616	$8,661
Eagle	$4,020	$1,152	$2,451	$7,623
Farraro	$1,782	$2,541	$1,237	$5,560
Gaire	$2,863	$400	$155	$3,419
Graft	$2,200	$1,060	$1,676	$4,935
Green	$26,774	$26,040	$20,585	$73,399
Hewlitt	$4,094	$4,447	$3,092	$11,633
Honeywell	$21,995	$9,530	$150	$31,675
IBM	$2,218	$3,494	$4,203	$9,914
Johnson	$21,122	$22,651	$7,784	$51,557
Luther	$38,035	$12,143	$3,268	$53,447
Orange	$7,736	$2,329	$7,464	$17,529
Osborne	$6,617	$1,365	$1,860	$9,841
Pear	$23,151	$17,779	$6,625	$47,556
Peters	$1,156	$248	$1,008	$2,412
Peterson	$2,104	$2,318	$2,432	$6,854
Reagan	$8,510	$2,294	$7,722	$18,526
Robin	$9,689	$2,541	$12,803	$25,033
Smith	$4,095	$3,753	$12,117	$19,966
Sparrow	$3,735	$3,624	$1,756	$9,115
Sperry	$3,640	$1,518	$2,101	$7,260
Stemper	$8,171	$2,953	$11,777	$22,902
Taylor	$5,631	$4,436	$2,989	$13,056
Wang	$5,384	$2,330	$4,696	$12,410
Washington	$3,678	$4,801	$3,689	$12,168
Weber	$2,104	$715	$1,245	$4,065
Total	$264,892	$152,694	$147,706	$565,292

	Salesperson Abbott	Salesperson Carlson
Total Profit	$14,943	($2,938)
Profit/Call per Client	$46	($17)

Figure 15–3a   Expenses per client and total profit per sales call—Plan 2.

Sls Calls $204	Expenses Other Marketing $232,700	G&A $10,000		
Sls Calls	Allocation OthlMktg	Overhead	Total Profit	Profit/Call
$4,080	$4,253	$183	$200	$10
$6,120	$5,023	$216	$834	$28
$16,320	$15,527	$667	$4,387	$55
$2,040	$581	$25	($1,363)	($136)
$8,160	$5,028	$216	$2,280	$57
$6,120	$3,792	$163	($1,414)	($47)
$6,120	$3,320	$143	($1,960)	($65)
$4,080	$2,281	$98	($899)	($45)
$4,080	$863	$37	($1,561)	($78)
$4,080	$2,247	$97	($1,488)	($74)
$10,200	$31,916	$1,372	$29,912	$598
$6,120	$4,988	$214	$310	$10
$8,160	$7,901	$340	$15,275	$382
$10,200	$5,229	$225	($5,739)	($115)
$20,400	$18,650	$801	$11,705	$117
$14,280	$14,782	$635	$23,749	$339
$4,080	$8,777	$377	$4,295	$215
$6,120	$3,426	$147	$148	$5
$8,160	$16,448	$707	$22,241	$556
$2,040	$1,186	$51	($865)	($86)
$2,040	$3,296	$142	$1,377	$138
$8,160	$9,147	$393	$826	$21
$16,320	$13,823	$594	($5,703)	($71)
$14,280	$12,479	$536	($7,329)	($105)
$4,080	$3,495	$150	$1,390	$69
$10,200	$3,065	$132	($6,137)	($123)
$6,120	$12,767	$549	$3,466	$116
$6,120	$5,217	$224	$1,495	$50
$12,240	$5,919	$254	($6,004)	($100)
$8,160	$5,532	$238	($1,761)	($44)
$4,080	$1,743	$75	($1,833)	($92)
$242,760	$232,700	$10,000	$79,832	$67

Current Year + 1		
Salesperson Holston	Salesperson Lewis	Salesperson Summers
$20,967	$36,260	$10,599
$54	$115	$46

pense columns is for sales calls. Each sales call has been arbitrarily budgeted at $204.00. As we saw in Figure 15-1, Holston, the salesperson for AT&T, estimated that he would need twenty sales calls for the new year, or $4,080, so this is the amount listed underneath sales calls for AT&T in the first column. Other marketing costs and G&A have been allocated on the basis of last year's expenditures as a percentage of sales.

AT&T's estimated total purchases of $119,764 (which also comes from Figure 15-1) are 1.8 percent of total estimated sales of $6,553,311. Multiplying 1.8 percent by total other marketing costs of $232,700 gives $4,253. This is the amount that is listed underneath other marketing for AT&T. The next column charges G&A; the same method is used for this as for other marketing costs. Now that expenses have been allocated by client, they can be subtracted from total gross profit to arrive at net profit by customer. The net profit shown for AT&T is $200.

When you know the total estimated profit by client or customer, you can calculate the estimated profit per sales call. This is shown in the last column of Figure 15-3a and a summary appears across the bottom of Figures 15-3 and 15-3a. You will notice that although Summers was projected to be number one in volume, he is not number one in either total profit or profit per sales call. Holston and Lewis are projected to deliver a higher total profit than Summers, with Summers and Abbott tied for number two in profit per sales call.

You will also notice in Figure 15-3a that several of the clients are showing a negative for total profit. Once again, if you analyze only volume, you cannot determine whether or not you are losing money servicing some customers. (This example uses clients or companies, but the same is true if your customer base is divided by markets.) Sales Plan 2 reveals that some clients are unprofitable, but it does not tell you which products/services sold to each customer or market are the losers.

For example, client Eagle, which is the seventh client from the top, accounts for $7,623 in total gross profit, but shows a -$1,960 in total profit. Quite possibly, one or more of the models are profitable. The question is which ones. This question is addressed in Sales Plan 3.

Forecasting by Net Profit by Customer by Product/Service (Plan 3)

Sales Plan 3 is similar to Plan 2 except that in Plan 3 expenses have been allocated to each individual product. This cost allocation is based on percentage of sales. These calculations are shown at the top of Figure 15-4.

Sales costs have not been previously allocated by product categories, so the total sales calls budget for the Northeast region as shown in Figure 15-3a ($242,760) has been allocated to each product at the same percentage (3.7 percent). This percent is arrived at by dividing the total sales budget by total sales ($6,553,311, as shown in Figure 15-1). G&A has been handled the same way. However, other marketing expenditures have been previously budgeted by product category, so last year's percent allocation has been used.

Let's use AT&T again for an example. Figure 15-2 contains sales estimates by product or model category (circuits, tubes, and valves). The sales estimate on circuits for AT&T is $25,778. To obtain the net profit on circuits sold through AT&T, you would multiply the $25,778 estimated sales volume by the gross margin of 17.06 percent. This would give you a gross profit of $4,399. This amount appears in the second column in Figure 15-4, in the row for AT&T. To obtain the net profit on circuits from AT&T, you would multiply the sales volume estimate of $25,778 by the cost allocation (based on a percentage of sales) for sales, other marketing, and overhead expenses. By

Figure 15–4   Net profit by product—Plan 3.

Cost Allocation:

	Total	Circuits		Tubes		Valves	
	Cost	Amount	%	Amount	%	Amount	%
Sales	$242,760	$57,501	3.70%	$53,412	3.70%	$131,846	3.70%
Other Mktg.	$232,700	$55,588	3.58%	$62,089	4.31%	$115,022	3.23%
G&A	$10,000	$2,369	0.15%	$2,200	0.15%	$5,431	0.15%
Total	$485,459	$115,458	7.44%	$117,701	8.16%	$252,299	7.09%

	Margins		
	17.06%	10.59%	4.15%

	Gross,			Net Profit			
Client	Circuits	Tubes	Valves	Circuits	Tubes	Valves	Total
AT&T	$4,399	$684	$3,632	$2,482	$157	($2,572)	$66
Amdahl	$5,404	$3,671	$3,118	$3,049	$841	($2,208)	$1,682
Apple	$20,886	$4,848	$11,168	$11,782	$1,111	($7,908)	$4,985
Bocuzzi	$595	$252	$435	$336	$58	($308)	$85
Bush	$9,384	$4,449	$1,851	$5,294	$1,020	($1,311)	$5,003
Commodore	$3,716	$2,329	$2,616	$2,097	$534	($1,852)	$778
Eagle	$4,020	$1,152	$2,451	$2,268	$264	($1,736)	$796
Farraro	$1,782	$2,541	$1,237	$1,006	$582	($876)	$712
Gaire	$2,863	$400	$155	$1,615	$92	($110)	$1,597
Graft	$2,200	$1,060	$1,676	$1,241	$243	($1,187)	$297
Green	$26,774	$26,040	$20,585	$15,104	$5,968	($14,576)	$6,495
Hewlitt	$4,094	$4,447	$3,092	$2,309	$1,019	($2,189)	$1,139
Honeywell	$21,995	$9,530	$150	$12,408	$2,184	($106)	$14,486
IBM	$2,218	$3,494	$4,203	$1,251	$801	($2,976)	($924)
Johnson	$21,122	$22,651	$7,784	$11,916	$5,191	($5,512)	$11,595
Luther	$38,035	$12,143	$3,268	$21,457	$2,783	($2,314)	$21,926
Orange	$7,736	$2,329	$7,464	$4,364	$534	($5,285)	($387)
Osborne	$6,617	$1,365	$1,860	$3,733	$313	($1,317)	$2,729
Pear	$23,151	$17,779	$6,625	$13,060	$4,075	($4,691)	$12,443
Peters	$1,156	$248	$1,008	$652	$57	($714)	($4)
Peterson	$2,104	$2,318	$2,432	$1,187	$531	($1,722)	($4)
Reagan	$8,510	$2,294	$7,722	$4,801	$526	($5,468)	($142)
Robin	$9,689	$2,541	$12,803	$5,466	$582	($9,066)	($3,017)
Smith	$4,095	$3,753	$12,117	$2,310	$860	($8,580)	($5,410)
Sparrow	$3,735	$3,624	$1,756	$2,107	$831	($1,243)	$1,694
Sperry	$3,640	$1,518	$2,101	$2,054	$348	($1,488)	$913
Stemper	$8,171	$2,953	$11,777	$4,610	$677	($8,340)	($3,053)
Taylor	$5,631	$4,436	$2,989	$3,177	$1,017	($2,117)	$2,076
Wang	$5,384	$2,330	$4,696	$3,037	$534	($3,325)	$246
Washington	$3,678	$4,801	$3,689	$2,075	$1,100	($2,613)	$563
Weber	$2,104	$715	$1,245	$1,187	$164	($882)	$469
Total	$264,892	$152,694	$147,706	$149,434	$34,993	($104,593)	$79,834

multiplying the total cost allocation of 7.44 percent by the total estimated volume of $25,778 and subtracting this total expense item from gross profit, you will receive net profit in the amount of $2,482. This amount appears in the fifth column in Figure 15–4 underneath net profit on circuits.

If you look across the bottom line in Figure 15–4 at the totals, you will notice that the net profit on circuits is projected at $149,434; on tubes, $34,993; and on valves a loss of $104,593. In other words, as the company is now operating, being in the valve business is costing it over $100,000 a year. As previously mentioned, the sad part about a situation like this is that most companies do not realize that one or more products/services are literally dragging down their total profit—and they are not aware of it because they do not calculate net profit by individual products or services.

Now, you may be thinking to yourself that it would be a great idea to break out expenses by product or service category, but you conclude that you cannot physically calculate these numbers. I would reply that you are copping out. Regardless of the product/service, it is not that difficult to allocate the costs or expenditures, especially when you take into consideration the 20/80 rule of thumb—that is, 20 percent of the activity, whether it be manufacturing or administration, probably accounts for over 80 percent of the total cost or expenditure. Therefore, just measure or monitor the manpower, machines, and so on that are used most extensively or are the most expensive and you will quickly get the figures you need.

Forecasting by Maximizing High-Potential Accounts (Plan 4)

As mentioned at the beginning of this chapter, the premise behind Plan 4 is that it should be no harder, and cost you no more, to go after the high-potential markets or customers than to pursue the average or below-average customer. IBM has been going to the data processing people in the large companies and saying, "I hear you have a problem." The data processing people say, "We sure do. We've lost control, because all our employees are going out into the marketplace and selecting their own PCs. In addition, when we have to tie all these PCs together or network them, we really are going to have a severe problem." What is the IBM salesperson's reply? Simple: She pulls out a contract for 200 IBM PCs and shows it to the data processing people. The IBM salesperson says that if they sign the contract, they will be back in control. They can pass out the IBM PCs to the employees, and when they have to network the system, it will be a piece of cake, because all the machines will be IBM. What are the data processing people going to do? Sign the contract, obviously. Meanwhile, the competitors' salespeople are spending an equal amount of time trying to sell one or two of their computers.

Our illustration of forecasting by maximizing high-potential accounts will be divided into five parts. They are:

1. Estimated sales potential and company development (Figure 15–5 and 15–5a)
2. Number of share points per marketing unit and cost per marketing unit (Figure 15–6)
3. Forecasting by maximizing high-potential accounts—circuits (Figures 15–7 and 15–8)
4. Forecasting by maximizing high-potential accounts—tubes (Figures 15–9 and 15–10)
5. Forecasting by maximizing high-potential accounts—valves (Figures 15–11 and 15–12)

Figure 15–5 contains estimated client total purchases by product category. Figure 15–5a indexes clients' purchases against the national average. For example, AT&T's total purchases for circuits for the new year are estimated at $122,776. This is only 57 percent of the national average. The national average (in this case, the Northeast region) is calculated by dividing the number of clients (31) into total estimated purchases ($6,682,266). This gives you the national average of $215,557. AT&T's total purchases are 43 percent below this national average. AT&T is also low in potential on tube purchases, with its total estimated purchases equaling only 18 percent of the national average. Its valve purchases are only 60 percent of the national average. Conversely, the second client listed, Amdahl, would be considered an extremely high-potential customer, because the estimated circuit volume is more than twice the national average, volume for tubes is 14 percent above the national average, and volume for valves, 27 percent over.

The third client, Apple, is similar to Amdahl, with total estimated purchases for each of the three product categories being considerably above the national average. By contrast, the fourth client, Bocuzzi, offers such low potential that it is literally impossible to handle this account at a profit. This does not mean that you should completely disregard customers that account for very small volume, especially if there is a possibility that they will increase their purchases in the future. The point is that you should not be servicing an account like Bocuzzi the same way you are servicing accounts such as Amdahl and Apple.

On the right-hand side of Figure 15–5a is estimated company sales by product category. These sales data have been picked up from Figure 15–2. As was done with client potential, company sales have also been indexed versus the national average. For example, estimated circuit sales to AT&T are approximately half of the national average for circuits, tube sales

Figures 15–5   Estimated sales potential—Plan 4.

		Client				
	Client Volume			**Index Natl. Avg.**		
Client	**Circuits**	**Tubes**	**Valves**	**Cir.**	**Tu.**	**Va.**
AT&T	$122,776	$34,667	$241,771	57%	18%	60%
Amdahl	$443,890	$224,778	$510,150	206%	114%	127%
Apple	$433,289	$224,779	$799,546	201%	114%	199%
Bocuzzi	$4,544	$7,566	$17,618	2%	4%	4%
Bush	$222,880	$332,779	$388,361	103%	169%	97%
Commodore	$122,440	$223,556	$366,009	57%	113%	91%
Eagle	$113,446	$22,990	$331,086	53%	12%	82%
Farraro	$34,889	$51,880	$170,193	16%	26%	42%
Gaire	$56,880	$134,667	$51,432	26%	68%	13%
Graft	$22,887	$25,677	$41,828	11%	13%	10%
Green	$336,778	$557,880	$1,673,366	156%	283%	416%
Hewlitt	$32,446	$56,779	$191,745	15%	29%	48%
Honeywell	$221,887	$227,665	$440,448	103%	116%	110%
IBM	$134,667	$109,887	$123,604	62%	56%	31%
Johnson	$668,997	$1,223,789	$1,608,721	310%	621%	400%
Luther	$1,567,443	$335,667	$872,246	727%	170%	217%
Orange	$221,889	$345,778	$668,257	103%	176%	166%
Osborne	$113,443	$156,776	$115,673	53%	80%	29%
Pear	$223,446	$228,990	$705,560	104%	116%	175%
Peters	$56,779	$35,664	$41,171	26%	18%	10%
Peterson	$43,447	$81,880	$43,439	20%	42%	11%
Reagan	$56,889	$102,778	$208,342	26%	52%	52%
Robin	$223,778	$134,667	$753,763	104%	68%	187%
Smith	$332,880	$443,778	$629,026	154%	225%	156%
Sparrow	$45,667	$32,556	$100,723	21%	17%	25%
Sperry	$223,556	$56,889	$151,071	104%	29%	38%
Stemper	$112,890	$198,770	$587,230	52%	101%	146%
Taylor	$134,889	$234,889	$364,778	63%	119%	91%
Wang	$210,897	$78,665	$127,191	98%	40%	32%
Washington	$123,889	$156,774	$108,802	57%	80%	27%
Weber	$17,788	$23,442	$34,292	8%	12%	9%
Total	$6,682,266	$6,107,302	$12,467,438	100%	100%	100%

are estimated to be only 14 percent, and valve sales, 76 percent. Company-estimated sales to Apple illustrate the opposite extreme. Both estimated circuit and valve sales are more than twice the national average.

Figure 15–5a Company development—Plan 4

| | Our Company | | | | |
| | Estimated Sales | | Index Natl. Avg. | | |
Sls. Cir.	Sls. Tu.	Sls. Va.	Cir.	Tu.	Va.
$25,778	$6,457	$87,529	51%	14%	76%
$31,667	$34,665	$75,126	63%	75%	65%
$122,388	$45,778	$269,118	244%	98%	234%
$3,489	$2,377	$10,484	7%	5%	9%
$54,990	$42,009	$44,604	110%	90%	39%
$21,778	$21,990	$63,033	43%	47%	55%
$23,556	$10,880	$59,068	47%	23%	51%
$10,445	$23,998	$29,797	21%	52%	26%
$16,778	$3,778	$3,742	34%	8%	3%
$12,889	$10,008	$40,378	26%	22%	35%
$156,897	$245,889	$496,022	313%	529%	432%
$23,990	$41,990	$74,505	48%	90%	65%
$128,890	$89,990	$3,620	257%	193%	3%
$12,996	$32,990	$101,277	26%	71%	88%
$123,776	$213,887	$187,563	247%	460%	163%
$222,886	$114,667	$78,750	445%	247%	69%
$45,332	$21,996	$179,857	91%	47%	157%
$38,776	$12,885	$44,812	77%	28%	39%
$135,665	$167,889	$159,644	271%	361%	139%
$6,775	$2,345	$24,284	14%	5%	21%
$12,332	$21,887	$58,602	25%	47%	51%
$49,867	$21,665	$186,075	100%	47%	162%
$56,779	$23,996	$308,498	113%	52%	269%
$23,997	$35,442	$291,982	48%	76%	254%
$21,886	$34,221	$42,313	44%	74%	37%
$21,331	$14,335	$50,637	43%	31%	44%
$47,884	$27,885	$283,787	96%	60%	247%
$32,997	$41,885	$72,029	66%	90%	63%
$31,552	$21,998	$113,151	63%	47%	99%
$21,553	$45,331	$88,902	43%	97%	77%
$12,332	$6,755	$30,002	25%	15%	26%
$1,552,251	$1,441,868	$3,559,192	100%	100%	100%

This indexing of estimated sales versus the national average is referred to as brand/service or company development.
Ideally, what you should be trying to accomplish through your
marketing efforts is to obtain above-national-average development in markets or companies that have above-average potential. That is another way of saying that your objective should be

to obtain a share in high-potential markets or accounts that is equal to or greater than your share in lower-potential markets or accounts.

The share objective for the Northeast region is 26 percent, as stated in Figure 15-1. This is a very good way to set a reasonable goal: your share of a particular high-potential client should equal your share of that market. Applying this share objective against AT&T's total estimated purchase of circuits in the amount of $122,776 yields $31,921. This approximates the sales estimate for AT&T, as shown in Figure 15-5. However, if we apply the 26 percent share goal against the total estimated purchases of circuits by Amdahl, this comes to $115,411. The company's current sales estimate is only $31,667. The question is, is it really that much more difficult to obtain a 26 percent share of the Amdahl business than to get 26 percent of the AT&T business? Not really—if you point these discrepancies out to your marketing people and then reward them on the basis of profit rather than volume.

Now that client potential as well as company development has been determined, the next question is, how much marketing pressure should be applied against each client, and what will be the cost? These questions are answered in Figure 15-6, which contains the second step we must take to maximize our high-potential customers.

The first part of Figure 15-6, Section A, shows how we determine the number of share points that should be obtained per marketing unit. A marketing unit, referred to in abbreviated form as MU, is an arbitrary amount of marketing weight. In this case history, the total number of estimated sales calls listed in Figure 15-1 has been used as the number for the total number of marketing units available. This figure is 1,190, as indicated on the first line under Section A in Figure 15-6. This number

Figure 15–6   Marketing units: share points, cost, and cost by cost component.

	Amount	Explanation
A. Number of share points per marketing unit (MU)		
Total MUs	1,190	Total number of sales calls (Fig. 15-1)
Number of customers	93	31 customer $\times$ 3 product lines
Average number of MUs per customer	12.8	1190/93
Total potential sales	$25,257,006	See Figure 15-1
Average product potential per customer	$271,581	$25,257,006/93
Average share objective	26%	See Figure 15-1
Average number of share points per MU	2.03	26%/12.8
B. Cost per MU		
Total sales costs	$242,760	See Figure 15-3a
Total other marketing costs	$232,700	See Figure 15-3a
Total G&A	$10,000	See Figure 15-3a
Total marketing/G&A	$485,460	$242,760 + $232,700 + $10,000
Cost per MU	$407.95	$485,460/1193
C. Cost per MU by cost component		
Sales	$204.00	$242,760/1190
Other marketing	$195.55	$232,700/1190
G&A	$8.40	$10,000/1190

could just as well have been 1,000, 10,000, or 500. It is an arbitrary figure that you use to:

1. Determine the number of units of marketing pressure that will be applied against each customer, market, or client.
2. Allocate marketing and other appropriate expenditures for each market or customer.

The next item is the number of customers. Here 93 has been used. The explanation is that there are thirty-one customers and three product lines; 3 times 31 equals 93. (The assumption is that each of the customers purchases each of the product lines.) This permits calculation of the average number of market units per customer, dividing the total number of marketing units available (1,190) by the number of customers (93) to reach 12.8, the weight of our MU.

The next line states total potential sales, and the answer is $25,257,006. This comes from Figure 15–1. Then comes another calculation, average product potential per customer. The answer is $271,581, this being the result of dividing $25,257,006 by 93. The average share objective follows; this is 26 percent, again lifted from Figure 15–1. With all the above information, you can now calculate the average number of share points that should be obtained per marketing unit, which is 2.03. This is simply 26 percent divided by 12.8.

To state this in another way, we have now determined the amount of marketing pressure that should be applied per share point in high-potential accounts. If the share objective is 26 percent, that will mean approximately thirteen sales calls (26 percent divided by 2.03) and thirteen units of other types of marketing effort that are being used. If the share objective is 10 percent, it will mean approximately five sales calls. And so on.

Here's a worksheet for you to calculate the number of share points per marketing unit for *your* company. It's really pretty straightforward if you go step by step. You can make a photocopy of this, or print out a copy from the Worksheets folder that you downloaded to your computer.

Worksheet 15–1　Number of share points per marketing unit

Total MUs _____

Number of customers _____

Average # of MUs per customer _____

Total potential sales _____

Average P/S potential per customer _____

Average share objective _____

Average # of share points per MU _____

Now that the number of share points per marketing unit has been determined, the next step is to calculate the marketing cost for each marketing unit. This is calculated under Section B in Figure 15–6. According to Figure 15–3a, total sales costs are estimated at $242,760, other marketing expenditures at $232,700, and G&A costs at $10,000. The sum of these figures results in a total marketing/G&A cost of $485,460, which is divided by number of MUs (1,190), to give a cost per marketing unit of $407.95. You will note that G&A costs have been included along with marketing. The reason for this is that it permits a calculation of net profit.

Use Worksheet 15–2 to calculate costs per marketing unit for *your* company.

Worksheet 15–2   Cost per marketing unit

Total sales costs _____

Total other marketing costs_____

Total G&A _____

Total marketing/G&A _____

Cost per MU _____

Section C of Figure 15–6 is a breakout of the cost of a marketing unit into sales, other marketing expenditures, and G&A. Worksheet 15–3 enables you to break out your cost per marketing unit by cost component.

Worksheet 15–3   Cost per marketing unit by cost component

Sales _____

Other Marketing _____

G&A_____

The preceding calculations give us sufficient data to apply the principle maximizing high-potential accounts. This is illustrated in the next three tables, with Figure 15–7 covering circuits; Figure 15–8, tubes; and Figure 15–9, valves.

In Figure 15–7, the first column lists the various clients, but unlike in the previous tables, the clients have been rearranged on the basis of their potential purchases of circuits. This is a numerical sort in descending order of the national average index from Figure 15–5. You will notice that the client Luther (how did that happen?) is estimated to have the highest potential on circuits, with an index of 727 percent, or seven times the national average. The next client, Johnson, has an index of 310 percent, which is three times the national average. Amdahl has an index of 206 percent, and so on. Clients Luther through Honeywell, which have an above-average potential, are listed at the top of the table, and clients with an index below 100 percent, or lower than the national average, are listed in the lower half.

The reason for this division is that two separate strategies will be used—one for above-average-potential customers and another for below-average-potential customers. The strategy for high-potential accounts is stated at the top of Figure 15–7, "Increase development to level of potential in high-potential accounts and allocate marketing and G&A expenses on basis of share objective." The strategy for low-potential accounts is stated in Figure 15–8: "No increase in sales in low-potential accounts and no marketing units against accounts where just one MU would generate a loss." The meaning of these two strategies will become clearer as the rest of the table is discussed.

Starting at the top, we see in Figure 15–7 that the first client listed is Luther. The second column shows estimated total circuit purchases, with the index (that is, potential circuits) shown in the third column. The fourth and fifth columns are on company

Figure 15-7 Above average potential—circuits.

Increase development to level of potential in high-potential accounts and allocate marketing and G&A expenses on basis of share objective.

| | Current | | | | | Revised | | | | | |
| | Client | | Company | | | | | | | | |
Client	Volume Circuits	Pot. Ctr.	Dev. Ctr.	Volume Circuits	Dev.	Volume	Share	Gross Margin 17.06%	Nb. of MUs (Share/2.0319 = MUs)	Total Cost of MUs @ $407.95	Revised Profit
Luther	$1,567,443	727%	445%	$222,886	727%	$364,108	23%	$62,117	11	$4,664	$57,453
Johnson	$668,997	310%	247%	$123,776	310%	$155,404	23%	$26,512	11	$4,664	$21,848
Amdahl	$443,890	206%	63%	$31,667	206%	$103,113	23%	$17,591	11	$4,664	$12,927
Apple	$433,289	201%	244%	$122,388	244%	$122,388	28%	$20,879	14	$5,671	$15,208
Green	$336,778	156%	313%	$156,897	313%	$156,897	47%	$26,767	23	$9,354	$17,413
Smith	$332,880	154%	48%	$23,997	154%	$77,326	23%	$13,192	11	$4,664	$8,528
Robin	$223,778	104%	113%	$56,779	113%	$56,779	25%	$9,686	12	$5,094	$4,592
Sperry	$223,556	104%	43%	$21,331	104%	$51,931	23%	$8,859	11	$4,664	$4,196
Pear	$223,446	104%	271%	$135,665	271%	$135,665	61%	$23,144	30	$12,190	$10,955
Bush	$222,880	103%	110%	$54,990	110%	$54,990	25%	$9,381	12	$4,954	$4,428
Orange	$221,889	103%	91%	$45,332	103%	$51,544	23%	$8,793	11	$4,664	$4,129
Honeywell	$221,887	103%	257%	$128,890	257%	$128,890	58%	$21,989	29	$11,663	$10,326
Total	$5,120,713	198%	187%	$1,124,598	243%	$1,459,034	28%	$248,911	188.52	$76,908	$172,003

development, with column four being the index and column five being the volume. The data for both these columns are picked up from Figure 15–5a. The sixth column contains the revised development objectives; the figure is picked up from either column three or column four, whichever is larger. For example, the revised development for Luther is shown as 727 percent, and this equals the potential index in column three. In the case of Apple, which is the fourth client down, the development objective is 244 percent, which is picked up from column four because the current company development is greater than the potential. An alternative way of stating this strategy on new development objectives is that sales goals will be equal to the client potential or current company development, whichever one is higher.

These new development objectives are used to calculate the revised sales volume, which is shown in column seven. The next column translates these volume figures into share, with the average share for high-potential accounts equaling 28 percent. The ninth column lists the gross margin. This figure minus the marketing-unit expenditure detailed in the next two columns results in the revised profit shown in the farthest column to the right.

Going back to the two columns between the gross margin and the revised profit, the one on the left details the number of marketing units to be used, and the one on the right states the total costs of the marketing units. For example, eleven marketing units will be used against Luther, because if you divide 2.03 into the 23 percent share objective, you will get 11. The total MU expenditure charged against Luther is eleven times the cost per unit ($11 \times \$497.95$).

All you have to do is look at the total revised profit for the high-potential clients on circuits alone, and you will realize what a dramatic effect this type of sales-development strategy can have on your bottom line. The total revised profit for both low- and high-potential clients, as shown in the very bottom row in the right-most column of Figure 15–8, is $175,891, which exceeds the total previous indicated profit for all three product categories against all thirty-one clients.

Figure 15–8 executes the strategy for low-potential clients, which, as stated above, is, "No increase in sales in low-potential accounts and no marketing units against accounts where just one MU would generate a loss." For example, clients Wang through Commodore can still offer profitable business, but clients Eagle through Bocuzzi are impossible to service without incurring a loss, because the cost of a marketing unit exceeds the gross profit generated by the resulting share points. For example, one marketing unit (one sales call, and so on) on a national average comes out to approximately a two share. A two share of the client potential on client Eagle is $2,268 ($113,446 × 0.02). The gross margin on $2,268 at the rate of 17.06 percent equals $387. This is less than the cost of a marketing unit, which is $407. This is not to say that in the real world you should completely eliminate clients such as Eagle through Bocuzzi, but it should indicate to you that you have to handle this type of business with a different strategy—maybe just telemarketing, or just brochures.

You can't solve a problem until you can spot it and only then develop new strategies. For example, Johns Hopkins University researchers were frustrated by the high school dropout rate. That was their problem. So they did research and found a high correlation between poor attendance of eight-graders and their subsequent dropout rate. Now the schools have special programs to help those with this profile.

Figures 15–9, 15–10, 15–11, and 15–12 are the same as Figures 15–7 and 15–8, except that they concern different product lines: tubes and valves. These exhibits illustrate that for these two products, no client below the national average in potential

(text continues on page 233)

Figure 15-8 Below average potential—circuits.

No increase in sales in low-potential accounts and no marketing units against accounts where just one MU would generate a loss.

| | Current | | | | | Revised | | | | | |
| | Client | | Company | | | | | | Nb. of MUs | | |
Client	Volume Circuits	Pot. Cir.	Volume Circuits	Dev. Cir.	Dev.	Volume	Share	Gross Margin 17.06%	(Share/ 2.0319 = MUs)	Total Cost of MUs @ $407.95	Revised Profit
Wang	$210,897	98%	$31,552	63%	63%	$31,552	15%	$5,383	7	$3,004	$2,379
Taylor	$134,889	63%	$32,997	66%	66%	$32,997	24%	$5,629	12	$4,911	$718
IBM	$134,667	62%	$12,996	26%	26%	$12,996	10%	$2,217	5	$1,938	$280
Washington	$123,889	57%	$21,553	43%	43%	$21,553	17%	$3,677	9	$3,493	$184
AT&T	$122,776	57%	$25,778	51%	51%	$25,778	21%	$4,398	10	$4,215	$182
Commodore	$122,440	57%	$21,778	43%	43%	$21,778	18%	$3,715	9	$3,571	$144
Eagle	$113,446	53%	$23,556	47%	0%	$0	0%	$0	0	$0	$0
Osborne	$113,443	53%	$38,776	77%	0%	$0	0%	$0	0	$0	$0
Stemper	$112,890	52%	$47,884	96%	0%	$0	0%	$0	0	$0	$0
Reagan	$56,889	26%	$49,867	100%	0%	$0	0%	$0	0	$0	$0
Gaire	$56,880	26%	$16,778	34%	0%	$0	0%	$0	0	$0	$0
Peters	$56,779	26%	$6,775	14%	0%	$0	0%	$0	0	$0	$0
Sparrow	$45,667	21%	$21,886	44%	0%	$0	0%	$0	0	$0	$0
Peterson	$43,447	20%	$12,332	25%	0%	$0	0%	$0	0	$0	$0
Farraro	$34,889	16%	$10,445	21%	0%	$0	0%	$0	0	$0	$0
Hewitt	$32,446	15%	$23,990	48%	0%	$0	0%	$0	0	$0	$0
Graft	$22,887	11%	$12,889	26%	0%	$0	0%	$0	0	$0	$0
Weber	$17,788	8%	$12,332	25%	0%	$0	0%	$0	0	$0	$0
Bocuzzi	$4,544	2%	$3,489	7%	0%	$0	0%	$0	0	$0	$0
Total	$1,561,553	38%	$427,653	45%	15%	$146,654	9%	$25,019	51.80	$21,132	$3,887
Gr. Tot.	$6,682,266	100%	$1,552,251	100%	103%	$1,605,688	24%	$273,930	240.32	$98,040	$175,891

Figure 15-9 Above average potential—tubes.

Increase development to level of potential in high-potential accounts and allocate marketing and G&A expenses on basis of share objectives

Client	Current				Dev.	Revised					
	Client		Company						Nb. of MUs (Share/ 2.0319 = MUs)	Total Cost of MUs @ $407.95	Revised Profit
	Volume Tubes	Pot. Tub.	Dev. Tub.	Volume Tubes		Volume	Share	Gross Margin 10.59%			
Johnson	$1,223,789	621%	460%	$213,887	621%	$288,923	24%	$30,597	12	$4,740	$25,857
Green	$557,880	283%	529%	$245,889	529%	$245,889	44%	$26,040	22	$8,849	$17,190
Smith	$443,778	225%	76%	$35,442	225%	$104,771	24%	$11,095	12	$4,740	$6,355
Orange	$345,778	176%	47%	$21,996	176%	$81,634	24%	$8,645	12	$4,740	$3,905
Luther	$335,667	170%	247%	$114,667	247%	$114,667	34%	$12,143	17	$6,859	$5,285
Bush	$332,779	169%	90%	$42,009	169%	$78,566	24%	$8,320	12	$4,740	$3,580
Taylor	$234,889	119%	90%	$41,885	119%	$55,455	24%	$5,873	12	$4,740	$1,133
Pear	$228,990	116%	361%	$167,889	361%	$167,889	73%	$17,779	36	$14,720	$3,059
Honeywell	$227,665	116%	193%	$89,990	193%	$89,990	40%	$9,530	19	$7,936	$1,594
Apple	$224,779	114%	98%	$45,778	114%	$53,068	24%	$5,620	12	$4,740	$880
Amdahl	$224,778	114%	75%	$34,665	114%	$53,068	24%	$5,620	12	$4,740	$880
Commodore	$223,556	113%	47%	$21,990	113%	$52,779	24%	$5,589	12	$4,740	$849
Stemper	$198,770	101%	60%	$27,885	101%	$46,927	24%	$4,970	12	$4,740	$230
Total	$4,803,098	188%	184%	$1,103,972	239%	$1,433,626	30%	$151,821	198.61	$81,024	$70,797

Figure 15-10 Below average potential—tubes.

No increase in sales in low-potential accounts and no marketing units against accounts where just one MU would generate a loss.

	Current — Client	Current	Company	Company	Company	Company	Company	Revised	Revised	Revised	Revised
Client	Volume Tubes	Pot. Tub.	Dev. Tub.	Volume Tubes	Dev.	Volume	Share	Gross Margin 10.59%	Nb. of MUs (Share/2.0319= MUs)	Total Cost of MUs @ $407.95	Revised Profit
Osborne	$156,776	80%	28%	$12,885	0%	$0	0%	$0	0	$0	$0
Washington	$156,774	80%	97%	$45,331	0%	$0	0%	$0	0	$0	$0
Robin	$134,667	68%	52%	$23,996	0%	$0	0%	$0	0	$0	$0
Gaire	$134,667	68%	8%	$3,778	0%	$0	0%	$0	0	$0	$0
IBM	$109,887	56%	71%	$32,990	0%	$0	0%	$0	0	$0	$0
Reagan	$102,778	52%	47%	$21,665	0%	$0	0%	$0	0	$0	$0
Peterson	$81,880	42%	47%	$21,887	0%	$0	0%	$0	0	$0	$0
Wang	$78,665	40%	47%	$21,998	0%	$0	0%	$0	0	$0	$0
Sperry	$56,889	29%	31%	$14,335	0%	$0	0%	$0	0	$0	$0
Hewett	$56,779	29%	90%	$41,990	0%	$0	0%	$0	0	$0	$0
Farraro	$51,880	26%	52%	$23,998	0%	$0	0%	$0	0	$0	$0
Peters	$35,664	18%	5%	$2,345	0%	$0	0%	$0	0	$0	$0
AT&T	$34,667	18%	14%	$6,457	0%	$0	0%	$0	0	$0	$0
Sparrow	$32,556	17%	52%	$24,221	0%	$0	0%	$0	0	$0	$0
Graft	$25,677	13%	22%	$10,008	0%	$0	0%	$0	0	$0	$0
Weber	$23,442	12%	15%	$6,755	0%	$0	0%	$0	0	$0	$0
Eagle	$22,990	12%	23%	$10,880	0%	$0	0%	$0	0	$0	$0
Bocuzzi	$7,566	4%	5%	$2,377	0%	$0	0%	$0	0	$0	$0
Total	$1,304,204	37%	39%	$327,896	100%	$1,433,626	23%	$151,821	198.61	$81,024	$70,797
Gr. Tot.	$6,107,302	100%	100%	$1,441,868	100%						

Figure 15–11 Above average potential—valves

Increase development to level of potential in high-potential accounts and allocate marketing and G&A expenses on basis of share objective.

	Current			Company			Revised					
Client	Volume Valves	Pot. Val.	Dev. Val.	Volume Valves	Dev.	Volume	Share	Gross Margin 4.15%	Nb. of MUs (Share/2.0319 = MUs)	Total Cost of MUs @ $407.95	Revised Profit
Green	$1,673,366	416%	432%	$496,022	432%	$496,022	30%	$20,585	15	$5,951	$14,634
Johnson	$1,608,721	400%	163%	$187,563	400%	$459,256	29%	$19,059	14	$5,732	$13,327
Luther	$872,246	217%	69%	$78,750	217%	$249,008	29%	$10,334	14	$5,732	$$44:6401 21
Apple	$799,546	199%	234%	$269,118	234%	$269,118	34%	$11,168	17	$5,732	
Robin	$753,763	187%	269%	$308,498	269%	$308,498	41%	$12,803	20	$8,217	$4,585
Pear	$705,560	175%	139%	$159,644	175%	$201,423	29%	$8,359	14	$5,732	$2,627
Orange	$668,257	166%	157%	$179,857	166%	$190,773	29%	$7,917	14	$5,732	$2,185
Smith	$629,026	156%	254%	$291,982	254%	$291,982	46%	$12,117	23	$9,319	$2,798
Stemper	$587,230	146%	247%	$283,787	247%	$283,787	48%	$11,777	24	$9,703	$2,075
Amdahl	$510,150	127%	65%	$75,126	127%	$145,637	29%	$6,044	14	$5,732	$312
Honeywell	$440,448	110%	3%	$3,620	110%	$125,739	29%	$5,218	14	$5,732	($513)
Total	$9,248,311	209%	185%	$2,333,968	239%	$3,021,243	33%	$125,382	182.22	$74,338	$51,043

Figure 15-12 Below average potential—valves.

No increase in sales in low-potential accounts and no marketing units against accounts where just one MU would generate a loss.

Client	Current Client Volume Values	Client Pot. Val.	Current Company Volume Values	Company Dev. Val.	Dev.	Volume	Share	Revised Gross Margin 4.15%	Nb. of MUs (Share/ 2.0319 = MUs)	Total Cost of MUs @ $407.95	Revised Profit
Bush	$388,361	97%	$44,604	39%	0%	$0	0%	$0	0	$0	$0
Commodore	$366,009	91%	$63,033	55%	0%	$0	0%	$0	0	$0	$0
Taylor	$364,778	91%	$72,029	63%	0%	$0	0%	$0	0	$0	$0
Eagle	$331,086	82%	$59,068	51%	0%	$0	0%	$0	0	$0	$0
AT&T	$241,771	60%	$87,529	76%	0%	$0	0%	$0	0	$0	$0
Reagan	$208,342	52%	$186,075	162%	0%	$0	0%	$0	0	$0	$0
Hewlitt	$191,745	48%	$74,505	65%	0%	$0	0%	$0	0	$0	$0
Farraro	$170,193	42%	$29,797	26%	0%	$0	0%	$0	0	$0	$0
Sperry	$151,071	38%	$50,637	44%	0%	$0	0%	$0	0	$0	$0
Wang	$127,191	32%	$113,151	99%	0%	$0	0%	$0	0	$0	$0
IBM	$123,604	31%	$101,277	88%	0%	$0	0%	$0	0	$0	$0
Osborne	$115,673	29%	$44,812	39%	0%	$0	0%	$0	0	$0	$0
Washington	$108,802	27%	$88,902	77%	0%	$0	0%	$0	0	$0	$0
Sparro w	$100,723	25%	$42,313	37%	0%	$0	0%	$0	0	$0	$0
Gaire	$51,432	13%	$3,742	3%	0%	$0	0%	$0	0	$0	$0
Peterson	$43,439	11%	$58,602	51%	0%	$0	0%	$0	0	$0	$0
Graft	$41,828	10%	$40,378	35%	0%	$0	0%	$0	0	$0	$0
Peters	$41,171	10%	$24,284	21%	0%	$0	0%	$0	0	$0	$0
Weber	$34,292	9%	$30,002	26%	0%	$0	0%	$0	0	$0	$0
Bocuzzi	$17,618	4%	$10,484	9%	0%	$0	0%	$0	0	$0	$0
Total	$3,219,127	40%	$1,225,224	53%	0%	$0	0%	$0	0	$0	$0
Gr. Tot.	$12,467,438	100%	$3,559,192	100%	85%	$3,021,243	24%	$125,382	182.22	$74,338	$51,043

can be handled profitably. The reason is that these gross margins are much lower than for circuits.

What Have We Learned?

Figure 15–13 is a summary of the four sales plans.

Figure 15–14 presents what is probably of greatest interest. It compares Plan 3 and Plan 4. It shows that total sales for Plan 4 are 8 percent lower than for Plan 3 and that gross profit is 2 percent lower. However, expenses for Plan 4 are 48 percent lower than for Plan 3, resulting in a net-profit increase of 273

Figure 15–13   The four sales plans.

Plan 1: Forecasting by Sales Volume by Customer

	Current Year	Current Year +1					Expenses			
	Sales	Sales	% +/–	Margin	Gross Profit	Number of Sales Calls	Sales	Other Mktg	G&A	Profit
Circuits										
Tubes										
Valves										
Total	$5,397,051	$6,553,311	21%			1,190				

Plan 2: Forecasting by Net Profit by Customer

	Current Year	Current Year +1					Expenses			
	Sales	Sales	% +/–	Margin	Gross Profit	Number of Sales Calls	Sales	Other Mktg	G&A	Profit
Circuits		$1,552,251		17.06%	$264,892					
Tubes		$1,441,868		10.59%	$152,694					
Valves		$3,559,192		4.15%	$147,706					
Total	$5,397,051	$6,553,311	21%	8.62%	$565,292	1190	$242,760	$232,700	$10,000	$79,832

Plan 3: Forecasting by Net Profit by Customer by Product

	Current Year	Current Year +1					Expenses			
	Sales	Sales	% +/–	Margin	Gross Profit	Number of Sales Calls	Sales	Other Mktg	G&A	Profit
Circuits		$1,552,251		17.06%	$264,892		$57,501	$55,588	$2,369	$149,439
Tubes		$1,441,868		10.59%	$152,694		$53,412	$62,089	$2,200	$34,993
Valves		$3,559,192		4.15%	$147,706		$131,845	$115,022	$5,431	($104,592)
Total	$5,397,051	$6,553,311	21%	8.62%	$565,292	1190	$242,758	$232,699	$10,000	$79,757

Plan 4: Forecasting by Maximizing High-Potential Accounts

	Current Year +1	Revised Current Year +1					Marketing Unit (MU) Expenses by Component			
					Gross		Sales	Other Mktg	G&A	
	Sales	Sales	% +/–	Margin	Profit	# of MUs	$204.00	$195.55	$8.40	Profit
Circuits	$1,552,251	$1,605,688	3%	17.06%	$273,930	240.32	$49,026	$46,994	$2,020	$175,891
Tubes	$1,441,868	$1,433,626	–1%	10.59%	$151,821	198.61	$40,517	$38,838	$1,669	$70,797
Valves	$3,559,192	$3,021,243	–15%	4.15%	$125,382	182.22	$37,174	$35,633	$1,531	$51,043
Total	$6,553,311	$6,060,557	–8%	9.09%	$551,133	621.16	$126,717	$121,465	$5,220	$297,731

Figure 15–14   Plan 3 versus Plan 4.

	Plan 3	Plan 4	+/–	Percentage
Total Sales	$6,553,311	$6,060,557	($492,754)	−8%
Gross Profit	$565,214	$551,133	($14,081)	−2%
Expenses				
Sales	$242,758	$126,717	($116,042)	−48%
Other Mktg	$232,699	$121,465	($111,234)	−48%
G&A	$10,000	$5,220	($4,780)	−48%
Total Expenses	$485,457	$253,402	($232,056)	−48%
Net Profit	**$79,757**	**$297,731**	**$217,974**	**273%**

percent for Plan 4 over Plan 3. The reason for the large decrease in expenditures is that the number of MUs has been cut from 1,190 to 621. This would require fewer sales personnel; the staff can be reduced through either transfers or attrition.

Worksheet 15–4, which ends this chapter, enables you to finish your own analysis of your client base. If you have already completed Worksheets 15–1, 15–2, and 15–3 to establish your MUs, then go ahead and fill out Worksheet 15–4 now. If you haven't, go back and do them first. If you don't know your clients' sales potential, assign that task to your sales force. The rest of the data you should have in house.

Worksheet 15–4 Forecasting by maximizing high-potential accounts

Product/Service _____

Client	Volume	Client Potential	Dev.	Company Volume	Dev.	Volume	Share	Gross margin	# MUs per share	Cost of MU	Revised profit
	——	——	——	——	——	——	——	——	——	——	——
	——	——	——	——	——	——	——	——	——	——	——
	——	——	——	——	——	——	——	——	——	——	——
	——	——	——	——	——	——	——	——	——	——	——
	——	——	——	——	——	——	——	——	——	——	——
	——	——	——	——	——	——	——	——	——	——	——
	——	——	——	——	——	——	——	——	——	——	——
	——	——	——	——	——	——	——	——	——	——	——
	——	——	——	——	——	——	——	——	——	——	——
	——	——	——	——	——	——	——	——	——	——	——
	——	——	——	——	——	——	——	——	——	——	——
	——	——	——	——	——	——	——	——	——	——	——
	——	——	——	——	——	——	——	——	——	——	——
	——	——	——	——	——	——	——	——	——	——	——
	——	——	——	——	——	——	——	——	——	——	——
	——	——	——	——	——	——	——	——	——	——	——

16 · The Internet Plan

In North America alone, over 250 million people connect to the Internet every day; globally, that figure is closer to 2 billion— and climbing. In order to compete in an economy that has become increasingly connected globally, effective use of the Internet and its various technological tools to market, advertise, and promote products and services is a necessity whether you're IBM, McDonald's, or a small local business—ready or not. In this chapter we cover the following: search engine optimization (SEO), pay per click (PPC), banner and pop-up ads, smartphones apps, and social media. SEO is particularly important because, unless you use outside media to promote your Internet site, you will only be "seen" if the search engines register your keywords. We show you how to optimize your keywords and offer a list of websites that will help you select the best ones for your business.

There are four basic types of websites—promotional, content-based, customer service, and transactional (i.e., sales)— but increasingly websites combine elements of each of the four basic websites into their websites. For example, on Verizon Wireless's website, you'll come across promotional information on their cellular offerings and special deals. Through their customer service component, you can pay your bill or find out how many minutes and text messages you've used. You can buy a new phone or a Bluetooth headset and have them shipped to your home. And you can find customer reviews of phones, as well as content on cell phone safety tips or how you can save money by bundling service offerings or other informational content. Amazon.com and countless other websites do the same.

Pay-Per-Click (PPC)

Pay-per-click programs are Internet advertising tools in which you, as an advertiser, pay a host or a search engine when their advertisement is clicked on by a web surfer. Generally whenever there's a pay-per-click arrangement on a website, the advertiser pays a fixed rate to the website/publisher. In many cases, the publisher/website has a rate card, much like a magazine, newspaper, or television network detailing how much it will cost to advertise within the website and it's based on several factors, including the popularity of that particular portion of the website. It's much more likely to be "pay *more* per click" on a segment of a website that's extremely popular and has a lot of traffic. Of course these rates can be negotiated if your business is planning to enter a long-term or high-value contract.

With search engines, it's much more likely for advertisers to bid on keyword searches relevant to their target market and to their business. In the bid-based model, the advertiser will sign a contract that allows them to compete against other advertisers in a private auction hosted by a publisher, an advertising network, or a search engine. Each advertiser informs the host of the maximum amount that he or she is willing to pay for a given ad spot, often based on a keyword. The auction plays out in an automated fashion every time a visitor triggers the ad spot whenever they use a search engine. When the ad spot is part of a search engine results page (SERP), the automated auction takes place whenever a search for the keyword that is being bid upon occurs. All bids for the keyword that target the searcher's geolocation (real-world location), the day and time of the search, etc., are then compared and the winner determined. In situations where there are multiple ad spots, a common occurrence on SERPs, there can be multiple winners whose positions on the page are influenced by the amount each company has bid. The ad with the highest bid generally shows up first, though additional factors such as ad quality and relevance can sometimes come into play. Bidding through a web engine may be an attractive way to market and advertise your company, your products, or your services to as large of an audience as possible. After all, almost every Internet user will use a search engine page—whether it's Google, Bing, or Yahoo!—at some point while online.

Banner and Pop-Up Advertising

Banner adverting consists of embedding your advertisement into a web page. You should place your banner ads on websites that have something in common with what you are selling. If your company manufactures washing machines and you place a banner ad on a website that sells computer parts, you probably won't have many readers clicking over to your website.

There are three ways you can promote your banner ad. You can pay the owner of the website you want to advertise on, you can exchange with others, and you can create your own "network," where you commission many sites to display your ad. DoubleClick (www.doubleclick.com), a subsidiary of Google, can help you with this.

If possible, you want to add movement or animation to your ad for greater effectiveness, as motion captures a viewer's attention. Several companies such as Corel (www.corel.com), ABC Banners (www.abcbanners.com), and Make Your Banner (www.makeyourbanner.com) can help you produce an effective banner ad.

But you should try to avoid making large expenditures on this kind of promotion. Banner ads have become less successful over the last decade or so, as many Internet users find them obtrusive, distracting, and irritating. And we have all grown increasingly wary of banner and pop-up ads, since some criminals use these methods to scam people or to pass on computer viruses.

Search Engine Optimization (SEO)

Search engine optimization involves the process of improving the visibility of a website or a web page on search engines by targeting different kinds of searches including image search, local search, video search, and industry-specific search engines. As search engines have gradually replaced the Yellow Pages and the White Pages, it has become increasingly necessary to employ SEO tactics for your business.

SEO as an Internet marketing strategy considers how search engines work and what people actually search for when they're online. Optimizing a website for searches can involve editing its content, as well as its HTML and other associated coding that make up the website and its design, to increase their relevance to specific keywords. This is also done to remove any barriers to the indexing activities of search engines. Generally, the earlier (or higher on the page) and more frequently a website appears in the search engine's results list, the more visitors it'll receive.

You cannot do this alone. A number of companies sell their services: www.seocentro.com/tools/search-engine/metatag-analyzer.html, wordtracker.com, and adwords.google.com/select/KeywordToolExternal are a few of the better known ones.

Cell Phones and Smartphones

At the end of 2009, roughly 21 percent of all American cell phone subscribers were using a smartphone such as the Blackberry, the iPhone, the Droid, and other models. Over the first few months of 2010, smartphone users have increased to about 29 percent of all cell phone subscribers. According to a recent Nielsen survey of cell phone users considering changing their phones or plans, 45 percent of respondents answered that they were considering some sort of smartphone as their next cell phone purchase. Based on these numbers and the falling prices of these devices, Nielsen projects that by the end of 2011, smartphones will overtake the standard phone market. Now that's increasing market share with a vengeance! Analysts are speculating that about 1 billion people globally will be using a smartphone by 2014. With such a growing trend, it will quickly seem imperative to consider marketing products and services through mobile devices, as these consumers will be accessing all sorts of specialized content on their phones.

Harris Interactive expects the entire mobile ad segment to become a $7.4 billion market by 2014. This even includes text messages. In a recent Harris survey, 40 percent of respondents said texting is extremely or very important. Clear Channel Communications in January 2010 sold out its inventory of certain mobile ads.

Consumer products marketers—food, beverage, liquor, fast-food restaurants, household cleaners, personal care, pet, and apparel brands, for example—have been at the forefront of using mobile apps to promote, market, and advertise their businesses. For many marketers, mobile apps have increasingly become part of an existing media strategy. In fact, in a December 2009 survey conducted by DM2PRO and Quattro Wireless, 64.8 percent of marketers and publishers reported planning to invest in mobile apps. Mobile phones and devices play an important role in consumers' lives and are spurring the growth of mobile apps.

Since many of these brands desire a closer relationship with consumers, mobile apps are ideal, because they offer—beyond the marketing message—the opportunity to invite these consumers into personal exchanges and much more immersive experiences. Of course if a brand is interested in developing a mobile app, they need to make sure that the app will be valuable to the user. There are now numerous mobile apps that fill utilitarian needs, serving up informative tips and educational bits; plenty that offer pure entertainment; and others that hover in between. For example, there are exciting new apps that enable you to reach your customers by mobile phone. Google has its "whisper"—targeted ads that will whisper your brand if the mobile users mention one of your keywords during a conversation. They also have an ad service that inserts your brand next to a search by a user. Foursquare brings up your store when the mobile user enters your area. Microsoft is channeling text-based ads on screens of phones using its upcoming Windows Phone 7 operating system, and Apple recently introduced the company's iAd platform.

Flipboard is a revolutionary iPad app for social news or even a personal newsstand. It turns Twitter and Facebook accounts into magazine look-alikes. It builds custom magazines from prebuilt curated boards or improved Twitter lists. And it works in reverse. A brand's Twitter account can be flipped to Flipboard.

Strategically, mobile apps may be appropriate for your company if your brand or company has a reputation for being a trendsetter. Plus companies will frequently jump at the chance to have regular, if not permanent, access to customers at just about any time and any place without the other distractions of Web 2.0. But this should only be done if your customer base sees themselves as trendsetters as well. Certainly, if being considered the first and best brand is part of your competitive advantage, then having a mobile app frequently creates powerful buzz among the social media world, as well as providing you with instant PR.

As brands are increasingly exchangeable, consumers are much more likely to quickly change brands multiple times. The mobile app is a closed environment for interaction between customers and brands in which brands can concentrate on the consumer dialogue—on the consumer's terms. Brands that want to keep their market position may also be interested in apps as a way to set a new standard to their competition, forcing the competition to catch up to the standard and even perfect it. In the world of Web 2.0 ideology nothing is perfect from the beginning. If something is missing, it can be optimized, adjusted, or set up anew—by the brand itself or by the community of the active consumers.

Executives who attended the Cannes Lions ad festival in 2009 told Reuters that emerging economics were also promising, though the lack of a global mobile phone standard could break a speedy development. "If you are interrupted every two minutes by advertising," says David Jones, global chief executive of Havas Worldwide, "not many people want that. The industry needs to work out smart and clever ways to engage people on mobiles."[1]

However, mobile advertising will likely attract interest from niche advertisers, which do not usually use mainstream media. They could shift ad budgets away from newspapers.

You should check out AdMob, Inc. (www.admob.com), if you are interested in advertising on cell phones. They sell ads across thousands of websites that are tailored for cell phones and were recently purchased by Google. Be careful, however: The ads are very small and the cell phone user can become annoyed.

WeReward can promote your business to smartphone users in your area. They use GPS to locate nearby potential customers and then send them ads on your facility. If the customer buys at your store, then he/she receives rewards from WeReward.

Social Media

Social media has revolutionized the Internet, how it's used, and how companies must market their services and products. Facebook, the website which expanded the social media revolution, now has over 400 million active users and recently became the world's most popular, most clicked website, beating out Google. "Marketers have always known that the best way to sell something is to get your friends to sell it," says Sheryl Sandburg, Facebook's chief operating officer. "That is what people do all day on Facebook. We enable effective word-of-mouth advertising at scale for the first time."[2]

Under the headline "Pepsi drops the Super Bowl to focus on Facebook," brandchannel.com's blogger Sara Zucker said, "Give Pepsi some credit. In addition to its efforts to offer consumers healthier options, the beverage behemoth also plans to forgo the Super Bowl to work on expanding into new media. . . . Pepsi is focusing its energy and money on its online presence where the brand believes a younger and accessible demographic is spending its time."[3]

That same blog quotes Ralph Santana, VP of marketing for PepsiCo North America: "We're living in a new age with consumers. They are looking for more of a two-way dialogue, story-telling and word of mouth. Mediums like the digital space are much more conducive toward that." Many companies are spending more advertising money on social media, because that is where the action is. Pizza Hut currently has over 25,000 followers on Twitter and over a million on Facebook. McDonald's has over 13,000 Twitter followers and 1,600,000 on Facebook.

Facebook is now offering a series of ad formats that tell users which of their Facebook friends have expressed interest in the brand or product featured in the ad. It is based on data it collects on the likes and friends of its users. The ad appears on the right side of a user's homepage, with an image and headline from the advertiser. With the ads are the names of any of the user's friends who have clicked on a button indicating they like the brand or ad.

Facebook had a 16.21 percent share of display-ad views in the United States in May 2010, up from 6.8 percent in January 2009, according to comScore, Inc., and Yahoo! is in second place with a 12.1 percent share. They have now commissioned Nielsen Company to measure ad performance. You can pay either by click or impression. You can go to the Facebook site and sign up for your ad. They will take you through the whole process including the design.

If your promotion campaign lends itself to video, the place to go is YouTube. Roughly 50 million users upload videos at an outstanding rate of twenty-four-hours worth of video every single minute, but millions more watch video clips daily. In fact, YouTube has quickly become the second most popular website and largest search engine in the world as more people go to YouTube than watch the Super Bowl. Their site, too, will take you through the complete process of becoming an advertiser. YouTube has signed up NPR, Politico, *The Huffington Post*, and the *San Francisco Chronicle* for YouTube Direct, a new method for managing video submissions from readers.

Branded entertainment on the web is gaining ground by the day: "The goal is to extend our reach," says Ellen Liu, media director at the Clorox Company in Oakland, California, "and attain a higher level of engagement than is possible through tactics like running 30-second commercials that interrupt episodes of conventional TV series."[4]

Twitter, the microblogging and social media site, is quickly gaining users and is constantly mentioned on the news. Many companies, like Best Buy, are constantly monitoring Twitter to determine what is being said about their stores and product offerings. Best Buy has their "Twelpforce" Twitter strategy where 500 people scout the site looking for persons who have questions about computers, television sets, etc. When a person tweets about a question on a product that Best Buy carries—or has a comment about Best Buy—invariably she will receive a tweet from a Best Buy representative. Here's a nice story: After buying a new navigational system at 6 A.M. on the most frenzied shopping day of the year, Laura S. Kern of Los Angeles could not figure out why it was not giving her traffic updates. She sent a message to Best Buy's Twitter account and within five minutes not one but *two* Best Buy employees responded with fix-it advice. Bet Ms. Kern is one of Best Buy's most loyal customers.

IBM and their agency, Ogilvy North America, used web searches, comments posted on YouTube, and conversations on Twitter to help develop their award-winning "Smarter Planet" campaign.

The Magazines Publishers of America is using Twitter to dispel the rumor that the Internet will drive magazines into extinction. It is running "The Twenty Tweetable Truths About Magazines," a campaign made up of factoids about the vitality of magazines. Various members post them on Twitter. The site is even being used by companies tweeting for hires as well as job seekers.

If you want links to your website on Twitter or from specific blogs, check out SponsoredReviews.com. They only charge $1.67 per link. And if you want bloggers to recommend your product or service, go to Mylikes.

Following is a worksheet for your objectives and strategies for the Internet with some objective suggestions. You can photocopy the worksheet here, or you can print out a copy from your downloaded Worksheets folder. You will probably need someone with Internet marketing experience to determine a realistic number of hits, clicks, etc., for your objectives.

Worksheet 16–1   Internet Plan: Objectives and strategies

Objectives

1. # of hits on SEO: _____

   _____

2. # of clicks on PPC: _____

   _____

3. # of clicks on Facebook: _____

   _____

4. # of clicks on Twitter: _____

   _____

Strategies

1. _____

   _____

2. _____

   _____

3. _____

   _____

4. _____

   _____

Notes

1. "Smart phones, social networks to boost mobile advertising," June 29, 2009; http://in.reuters.com/article/idINLT63327920090629.

2. Emily Steel and Geoffrey A. Fowler, "Facebook Touts Selling Power of Friendship," *Wall Street Journal*, July 7, 2010; http://online.wsj.com/article/SB10001424052748704545004575353092563126732.html.

3. Sarah Zucker, "Pepsi Drops Super Bowl to Focus on Facebook," February 1, 2010; http://www.brandchannel.com/home/post/2010/02/01/Pepsi-Drops-Super-Bowl-To-Focus-On-Facebook.aspx.

4. "Clorox, ConAgra, Maybelline Deals Signal Resurgence in Web Series Interest," PlaceVine, November 24, 2009; http://www.placevine.com/blog/2009/11/24/clorox-conagra-maybelline-resurgence-in-interest-for-web-series/.

17 · The Research Plan

You have noticed at the end of each chapter on a marketing component, I have inserted a copy of the Word document into which you insert your objectives and strategies for each part of the marketing plan. These objectives should be written so they are measurable—because unless they are measurable, you cannot monitor them. I believe a plan that is not monitored is not a plan, but just a wish list. You want to monitor your plan every few weeks and make changes if you are off target. Don't wait until the end of the plan year to check your progress because you may have wasted most of the year by so doing.

You can monitor several of your measurable objectives in-house. Some of these are your number of sales leads, presentations, and closure rate; Internet clicks; reach and frequency; and customer service and public relations activities. To monitor other types of objectives such as your customer analysis, pricing, sales forecasting, and product/service objectives, you may need some outside help.

You could definitely order a benchmark study in which an outside research company can pose questions to your current and potential customers. To test your print advertising, you can use companies such as Starch Research (www.starchresearch .com) and for broadcast advertising, Ipsos ASI Research (www .ispos-asi.com). Focus groups can also be used to find answers to some questions, and although they can be more limited than a benchmark study, they are frequently less expensive. And of course, there is the Internet. Each of these methods will be discussed in the following sections.

In-House Activities

Some marketing people are unaware of all the market data buried within a company, so your first step is to ask around about what is available. Your own marketing department may be a treasure trove. You also want to check with trade associations, trade journals, and the federal government. The federal government has more research data than all the research companies combined. The trick is finding where it is. There is also a ton of information available on the Internet.

Benchmark Studies

Most survey research simply involves surveys among a representative sample of individuals. Very carefully designed questionnaires, usually administered in a structured manner, are used to guide the interview. They could be about attitudes, needs, or preferences. The questions could be "closed-end" (for example, "yes" or "no") or they could be "open-ended" ("What do you think of . . .?"). There are no right or wrong answers in survey research. You can find research companies by checking the Council of American Survey Research Organization's (www.casro.org) more than 325 members and using their member directory: You insert your market, description of potential customers, and what type of benchmark study you desire, and a selection of appropriate organizations will be presented to you.

There are several types of benchmark studies: personal interviews, telephone, mail, and e-mail. Personal interviews are the most effective because you can ask more questions, the interviewer can probe and ask follow-up questions, and you can show graphics. The disadvantages are that they are the most expensive and take the most time to complete the study. Telephone interviews can save you time and money, but you have to ask fewer questions and you can't show graphics. Interviews by mail cost the least of the three "nondigital" methods, but the disadvantages are the low rate of return, and the returns may not represent the universe of respondents you are interested in.

You can also turn to the Internet for your surveys. The Internet allows you to send surveys via e-mail to large numbers of potential participants who can then fill out the surveys on their own time—if they choose to fill them out. These surveys frequently contain similar material to that of surveys done by companies such as Starch, Roper, and Ipsos ASI. The Internet surveys can ask a variety of questions on a particular subject or product offering. For example, the National Basketball Association, Major League Baseball, and the National Hockey League have electronic surveys asking fans all sorts of questions including their feelings and thoughts on that league's particular ad campaign, on that league's particular broadcasts, which teams fans like, how often fans go to games, and what fans would prefer to see and do at the game—and more.

You can use a benchmark study to help determine the size of your market, your market share, perception of your price, your complete customer analysis, perception of your business, perception of competition, and other answers you need for your fact book and to measure your objectives.

Advertising Research

Figure 17-1 is a flow chart on creative development that I showed you in Chapter 9, The Advertising Plan. It shows you the different points in the strategy development process you need to text. It's vital that you understand the importance of testing your advertising concepts.

You can obtain information on benefits sought and benefits delivered from your benchmark study. You can also test your

Figure 17–1   Creative development testing timeline.

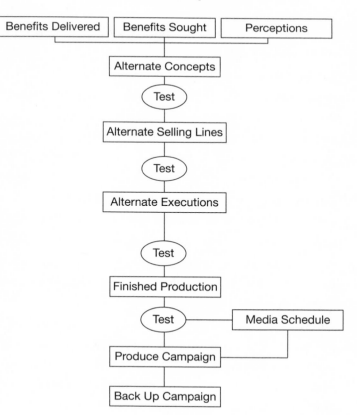

various concepts by drawing them on some 8½-by-11 inch sheets of cardboard and passing them on to the interviewee like a deck of cards. You then ask about their perception of each card (or screen, if you are doing this electronically).

Research on Your Print Campaign

Starch Research, Roper Canada, Ipsos ASI, and many other companies provide valuable research on your print advertising. These research companies offer surveys conducted by means of personal interviews with readers of specific issues of newspapers, consumer magazines, and business and professional publications.

The first objective of any ad is to be noticed. Any research firm measures this fundamental aspect of advertising performance, as well as measuring the ad's ability to communicate brand association, and the extent of reader involvement in copy reading. These measures—noting, brand association, and read most—are reported for each ad in a particular magazine issue. This permits a useful context for evaluation, as ad effectiveness is related to scores for other ads of the same size, color, and product category.

Ad norms or averages for specific titles provide a further performance benchmark. Track your own campaign, measure competitive advertising, and learn which elements contribute to high readership scores.

All print advertisements are designed to meet specific communication objectives. Yet few ads are independently evaluated to determine whether the intended message is being conveyed. In fact, some ads inadvertently communicate undesired messages.

These research companies also can provide advertisers with evidence of advertising effectiveness and the return on their advertising investment. Typically, these studies will evaluate each advertisement on the basis of its creative elements (interest, innovation, visual appeal, and attention value) as well as its content elements (clarity, information value, believability, and persuasiveness). Additionally, communication value, relevance, attitude to the product or advertising, and the amount of information contained within the ad will be measured in these studies. An extensive database of norms will provide the context for evaluation.

One or more concept ads are evaluated to help advertisers determine the most effective combination of visuals and copy to achieve the desired communication objectives. Test ads are inserted into a mocked-up magazine or newspaper that respondents are asked to leaf through. Questions are posed concerning ad recall on an unaided, partly aided, and prompted basis. Respondents are asked to read the test ad thoroughly and a diagnostic test is administered.

Research for an Internet Campaign

A source for Internet research you want to check out is emarketer.com. According to Paul Iagnoco, director of global digital strategy at Kellogg's, "With its articles, charts, and analysis, eMarketer is a whole library of resources for us. eMarketer is the authority—it validates trends and gives credibility to what we're proposing."

Another is doubleclick.com. The company's research team can offer clients deep insights on industry trends, as well as performance metrics and benchmarks. It provides custom campaign analyses, manages individual client-driven research projects, and offers training and best practices presentations and sessions.

A new company by the name of Omniture (www.omniture

.com) delivers its customers traffic data as it happens in real time, tracking everything from how many people visit a website to where they're coming from to how long they linger. Google and some hosting services provide the same information. Quantcast (www.quantcast.com) allows you to obtain the demographics of visitors to your site and can now also place you on sites that meet your demographics.

Below is a worksheet for your research plan objectives and strategies, which you can photocopy or print out from your downloaded folder of worksheets. This is where you list all your measurable objectives from other parts of the plan and spell out how you are going to monitor them. Be sure you put numbers in your objectives so you can keep measuring whether or not you are hitting your target. If you are not on target, then you should consider changing your strategies.

Worksheet 17–1   Research plan: Objectives and strategies

Objectives

1. _____
   _____
2. _____
   _____
3. _____
   _____
4. _____
   _____
5. _____
   _____
6. _____
   _____

Strategies

1. _____
   _____

2. _____
   _____

3. _____
   _____

4. _____
   _____

5. _____
   _____

6. _____
   _____

18 · Pulling the Plan Together

What I recommend you do first is to go back through the various case histories. Change numbers here and there to see what happens to the overall goals or objectives of each file (you can even save your "trysies" with different names). Play around. Get familiar with each of them. When you feel comfortable with the case study files, open up the software with the files for your data and start inserting some facts or numbers and then complete your objectives and strategies. You can start with any file, but I suggest you follow the book.

On customer analysis (see Chapter 4), what you are looking for is who really makes the buying decision and what turns them on. You don't start by describing what your product or service does, but what it will do for the prospective buyer. You don't buy roses for your better half because they are beautiful. You buy them in the hopes that you will get a kiss.

In Chapter 6 (The Product/Service Plan) I gave you the choice of four different mousetraps to trap your customers. Your business needs a personality. A uniqueness. You want to be a Marriott. A Wal-Mart. Not a General Motors, which has a blah personality due to their financial problems and boring advertising.

In Chapter 7 (Caculating Your Marketing Communications Budget), you were provided with worksheets to help you calculate a budget, and in Chapter 8 (Competitive Analysis), the worksheets help you compare your product/service to those of your competitors.

In the chapter on advertising (see Chapter 9), I refer to the creative strategy. This is a critical document because if you do not have one, there will be no continuity in your message to customers. You should have one message for each prospect at the top of the purchase process, whether you are making a sales presentation, staffing a booth at a trade show, or sending some advertising in his or her direction. If you are going after a CEO, engineer, or housewife, each has a different benefit that turns him or her on. Find that benefit and that should be the only message to that particular job description or lifestyle. You also want to calculate your reach and frequency to be sure you have the right weight in your advertising expenditures.

Be sure you take advantage of all the facets of sales promotion (see Chapter 10). Once again, be unique. Bring in a fifteen-foot-tall end-of-aisle display into your retail outlets. Be sure it's animated. Offer a 25 cent coupon on your $20,000 pieces of equipment. Check to see if the cost of your trade shows, bingo cards, and catalogs are less than the amount of profit they deliver.

Remember, a favorable publicity story on your business is worth several ads (see Chapter 11). If one company can get expansive news coverage on just adding a new department to their store, you can't cop out by saying you have nothing interesting to write about. And tie-ins with charity have been very successful for several companies.

As I said in Chapter 12, The Sales Plan: Pricing, *please* do not add up your costs and then add an arbitrary markup. You are not looking at the price that gives you the greatest volume or the greatest unit margin. You want the price that gives you the greatest margin in total dollars.

In determining future sales (see Chapter 13), once again do not use an arbitrary growth percentage. Although this file is quite large, it takes into account all the factors that will determine your future sales and profit. You will need some research here, as you will to get the data you need for some of the other files, but it is information you need if you are going to be a professional planner.

Tell everyone in your company that customer service is not a department, but an attitude (see Chapter 14). Weren't you impressed when you called a business and a live person answered on the first ring? I don't care if that receptionist costs that company $100,000 per year; she was more than worth it. Keeping a customer only costs one-fifth as much as acquiring a new one.

The Internet is a whole new ball game, especially social media. If you're going to use the Internet to get customers—and in today's world, that's pretty much of a must!—do so sensibly. Get in touch with some of the websites I mention in Chapter 16, and move cautiously. You may want to hire your own consultant to guide you.

After going through the Excel files inserting your data, the next step is to contact a research company to help you confirm your data and fill in any blanks. Contact a research company that will do a benchmark study (see Chapter 17) for you and show them all the data you inserted into the software files. They will then give you a proposal for a study.

After you complete your research, you should be able to finish inserting your own company data into the software cells for:

1. Customer analysis
2. Experience curve
3. Reach and frequency
4. Trade
5. Pricing
6. Sales forecasting

All this information belongs in your fact book and it supports your objectives and strategies. You also should have completed your objectives and strategies in the Word files for the:

1. Product/service plan
2. Advertising plan
3. Sales promotion plan
4. Public relations plan
5. Sales plan
6. Customer service plan
7. Internet plan
8. Research plan

All of these plans belong in your marketing plan, along with your:

1. Positioning strategy
2. Creative strategy
3. Marketing communications budget
4. Competitive analysis
5. Maximizing the high-potential accounts

In addition, you may want to add some *overall* objectives and strategies. Your overall objectives could cover factors such as profit and market share and your overall strategies could deal with your company-wide positioning. Worksheet 18–1 follows. You can photocopy it, or print out a copy from your downloaded Worksheets folder.

Worksheet 18–1 Marketing plan: Overall objectives and strategies

Objectives

1. _____

2. _____

3. _____

4. _____

Strategies

1. _____

2. _____

3. _____

4. _____

Print out copies of all your completed files and you are done. Hooray! Remember to keep self-inspecting and using research to continuously monitor your plan.

Appendix A
Marketing Plan Basics

This document will provide you with a handy summary of how to prepare your own marketing plan, all of which was discussed in detail in this 4th edition of *The Marketing Plan*. We will present the following topics in abbreviated, outline form.

Section I: Strategic Position, Marketing Personnel, Fact Book Summary, and Major Marketing Objectives and Strategies
Section II: Product/Service Plan
Section III: Marketing Communications Plan
Section IV: Research Plan
Section V: Customer Service Plan
Section VI: Sales Management Plan
Section VII: Budget, Timing, Plans, and Action Plans

Section I: Strategic Position, Marketing Personnel, Fact Book Summary, and Major Marketing Objectives and Strategies

Strategic Position

1. Relative profit potential of this market within the company. Example: a new market with the highest profit

potential of all markets in which the business is currently competing.

2. Critique on company versus competition as to current status as well as ability to acquire the critical business strengths needed to become a major player in this market.

3. Definition of strategic position and payout. Example: Strategic position will be to go for maximum market share and become market leader with a break-even in five years.

Marketing Personnel

1. State which components of the business are involved in the marketing function.

2. If you employ an advertising agency, state its role in the preparation of the plan.

3. State the name of the planning leader for the plan, the members of the planning team, the individual who is responsible for keeping the fact book up to date, and the individuals responsible for monitoring the various sections of the plan to be sure the strategies are executed correctly and the objectives are met.

Fact Book Summary

1. Statement on marketing aspects of the market.
2. Statement on marketing strength of competition.
3. Definition of target audience.
4. Delineation of company marketing strengths and weaknesses for competing in this market.

Major Marketing Objectives

1. Market share objectives.
2. Distribution and depth of line objectives.

3. New product/service introduction objectives.
4. Awareness, preference, and sales closure rate objectives.
5. Repeat purchase rate and volume/profit per purchase objectives.
6. Marketing budget and timing.
7. Gross sales, gross margin, operating margin, and net profit objectives (sum of all functional plans: R&D, engineering, manufacturing, operations, marketing, and G&A).
8. Return-on-investment (ROI), return-on-assets (ROA), return-on-net-assets (RONA), and/or discounted cash flow (DCF) objectives (sum of all functional plans).

Major Marketing Strategies

1. Positioning statement. Example: Position the brand in the segment of the market of consumers who desire more preprogrammed options, thus extending the use and value of the brand. This target is the numbers-oriented person (e.g., the engineer, aviator, accountant, or retailer).
2. Distribution strategy. Example: Position the brand among dealers as the most attractive service to the above-mentioned target, one that is not currently being reached by brands Able and Baker and thus not a duplication of inventory. Develop in-store merchandising units to demonstrate and allow consumer to "work" new model, thereby reinforcing brand difference at point of sale.
3. Communications strategy. Example: Thrust of marketing communications will be consumer "pull" rather than dealer "push." Dealer push is when you sell on price. Build brand awareness and recognition of brand

difference with target consumer, first through specialized media and later through mass media.

4. Pricing strategy. Example: Price competitively with major competition.

Section II: Product/Service Plan

Product/Service Plan Objectives

1. Set objectives for subjects such as allocation of marketing dollars per product/service, distribution, depth of line, packaging, pricing, awareness, preference, and repeat purchasing.
2. Examples:
   a. Model 1040 and 1041 will receive 90 percent of marketing dollars due to higher profit margins.
   b. Increase the average price to $1,961 on models 1040 and 1041.
   c. Expand distribution among chains from 29 percent to 50 percent, among department stores from 50 percent to 75 percent, and among independents from 17 percent to 35 percent.
   d. Reduce packaging costs to $2.50 for chains, $2.25 for department stores, $1.50 for owned and operateds (O/O), and $3.00 for independents.

Product/Service Plan Strategies

1. Set one or more strategies for each objective.
2. Examples:
   a. All advertising and sales promotion will feature models 1040 and 1041. In addition, sales force will receive double bonus points on these two models.

   b. Prices will be raised for O/Os and independents to $2,100, coupled with the company's pledge for greater advertising support. Chain and department store pricing will remain the same.

   c. Major expansion in distribution will be obtained through a 35 percent increase in the sales force and a 25 percent increase in the communications budget.

   d. The new technology on vacuum packaging developed last year by R&D will be used for all models within the next two years.

Product/Service Plans

1. Develop at least one plan for each above strategy. The plan states how you plan to execute the strategy.
2. Summarize the plan in the marketing plan and put the data in action plans. The action plan should include each step or task, who is responsible for each step or task, and the date by which each step or task has to be completed. If the strategy is to use trade shows to accomplish a certain objective, then the action plan should delineate each step necessary to execute the strategy, including selecting the shows, booking the space, designing the exhibit, and determining who will attend.

Section III: Marketing Communication Plan

Marketing Communications Plan Objectives

1. Include objectives on advertising, sales promotion, and public relations.
2. Advertising Plan examples:
   a. Among senior data processing professionals in companies with sales over $20 million: increase

awareness of Ryan minicomputer from 30 percent to 50 percent; increase association with major selling point (more data storage per dollar) from 25 percent to 40 percent.

b. Among dealers of small computer systems, increase awareness of brand.

3. Sales Promotion Plan examples:
   a. Demonstrate high-impact resistance of new housing on energy monitor to 300 design engineers.
   b. Reduce sales time necessary to educate purchasing agents on specifications of thermocoupler line from an average of ninety minutes to thirty minutes.
   c. Generate $50,000 in direct sales of replacement parts.
   d. Reduce the number of unqualified leads sent to the sales force by 50 percent.

4. Public Relations Plan examples:
   a. Placement of two major articles in general business, news magazines, or Internet.
   b. Placement of major article on new Series 100 line in every data processing publication.

Marketing Communications Plan Strategies

1. Set one or more strategies for each above objective.
2. Advertising Plan examples:
   a. Creative strategy:
      i. Major benefit: more data storage per dollar.
      ii. Copy points: Competitively priced; offers twice the number of circuits per chip; supports 30 percent more sectors per track versus competition.
   b. Media strategy:
      i. Reach 65 percent of senior data processing professionals in companies with sales over $20 million

with a frequency of eight over a twelve-month period.

    ii. Concentrate all media dollars in the leading trade vertical magazine, adding second magazine in the field only if necessary to reach required reach.

3. Sales Promotion Plan examples:

    a. To demonstrate impact resistance of new housing, take a booth in July WESPLEX show and design exhibit offering a prize to anyone checking housing with sledge hammer. Publicize exhibit and prize by direct mail to design engineers.

    b. Review brochures on thermocoupler line to incorporate complete specifications and clear explanation to differences between each item in the line.

    c. To build direct sales program for replacement parts, start with list of customers with models between the ages of three and five. Set up system of twenty-four-hour handling of orders. Stress that fast service results in less downtime for customer.

4. Public Relations Plan examples:

    a. Use lure of exclusive sneak preview of Series 100 line and/or set up exclusive interview with CEO for major business/newsweekly article.

    b. Fly in editors of all data processing publications for preview of Series 100 three months before introduction to secure major coverage in their May editions.

Section IV: Research Plan

Research Plan Objectives

1. Set objectives for methods you will use to measure the effectiveness of your marketing plan, changes in the market, and new product/service development.

2. Examples:
   a. Conduct a statistically projectable study of the target audience to obtain current levels on awareness, registration of selling message, preference, and intent to buy.
   b. Determine needs of the company's customers and the current ranking of the company's customer service department concerning the competition.
   c. Determine two leading benefits of new model 707 to the aircraft instrumentation industry.

Section V: Customer Service Plan

Customer Service Plan Objectives

1. Set objectives for the performance of customer service (e.g., effectiveness ranking within the industry, management involvement, marketing involvement, knowledge of product/service line, number of telephone rings before response, cost of handling returns, and expertise of technical personnel).
2. Examples:
   a. Company will be ranked number one in the industry in customer service effectiveness within two years.
   b. All phones will be answered by the third ring.
   c. Customer service personnel will have access to all marketing information available to product mangers.

Customer Service Plan Strategies

1. Set one or more strategies for each objective.
2. Examples:
   a. All customer service personnel will be given a free weekend trip to either Disneyland or Disney World to permit them to observe the finest customer service organization in the world.

b. An independent company will be commissioned to answer any customer service phone after two rings. The customer service department will be charged the complete cost, which will be deducted from customer service employees' bonuses.

c. All customer service personnel responsible for product/service knowledge will have access to a database that will allow them to bring up any type of information on any product/service sold by the company.

Section VI: Sales Management Plan

Sales Management Plan Objectives

1. Set objectives on subjects such as sales goals per product/service line, sales closure rate, cost per sales call, number of sales calls per day, and sales training.

2. Examples:

    a. Maintain current field force of twenty people on service A and increase sales from $910,113 to $995,000.

    b. Increase average sales closure rate from current 22 percent to 28 percent.

    c. Average 20 percent of sales force calls by field force on service B to frequent travelers to speed up penetration of this market.

    d. Increase division profitability by increasing sales of service C from 30 percent to 35 percent.

Sales Management Plan Strategies

1. Set one or more strategies for each objective.

2. Examples:

    a. Improve field sales force productivity on service A through a combination of efforts including forming home office unit with 1-800 telephone number lines to take over customer tracking and routine reorders and creating series of direct-mail pieces to qualify inquiries before sending to field.

b. To increase closure rate, a minimum of one-third of the entire sale force will be sent to a new one-week session for sales training that will incorporate a new concept of "town meeting" dialogue to improve each individual's ability to close.

c. To increase penetration of service C, hire ten new salespeople to work as task force rolling out service as each new region is targeted.

d. To increase proportion of sales of service C, create bonus compensation plan based on points awarded according to margins on various services.

Section VII: Budgets, Timing, Plans, and Action Plans

Budgets

All objectives should be measurable to enable you to determine whether you meet them. That means they require a goal, a control, and timing or date. In the preceding pages there are several examples of objectives with goals. Put the control (usually the amount of money to be spent) or the budget in each objective, or you can put the control for each objective in summary form at the end of the plan.

After you have approved goals and controls, monitor them each week to be sure you are on target. If you are off target sometime during the year, you have to change either the goal or the control or alter the strategy.

Timing

Timing refers to the date by which the objective must be achieved. Like controls, the timing can be inserted in each objective or can be summarized at the end of the plan. Like controls, timing has to be continuously monitored.

Plans

Plans are the execution of the strategies. They should be summarized in the marketing plan. After the complete marketing plan is approved, action plans should be written to provide the details. If you include all the details of executing a strategy in the marketing plan itself, you may be confronted with three possible problems:

1. You end up with a 50- to 200-page document that no one will read, and the plan just gathers dust on the shelf.
2. If the plan is not approved, you have wasted time developing all the details.
3. Using a separate action plan lets the people who will actually execute the plan decide for themselves how they should do it.

Action Plans

An action plan contains the detailed execution of one or more strategies and should include at least three factors:

1. Each necessary step or task
2. Who will be responsible for accomplishing each step or task
3. The required completion date of each step or task

For each marketing plan, you may have between five and twenty action plans. The sum of all your action plans are your milestone calendar or perk chart. A milestone calendar keeps you on target relative to timing. A perk chart determines which completion dates for certain steps or tasks are the most critical and have to be watched most closely. These critical steps or tasks are the ones that influence the beginning of another step or task.

Keep your action plans in separate documents. Your fact book should also be in a separate binder. This will enable you to have a short, concise, operational marketing plan that you can refer to each week. If your marketing plan is not operational, the preparation is nothing more than an exercise. These documents can also be on your server, with all employees having access through their own computer.

Appendix B
Everything You Need to Know About
Working with an Advertising Agency

I. Working with advertising agencies:
   A. Relationship should be as business partner, not adversary.
   B. Recognize the business versus creative conflict.
   C. Recognize that the account representative is usually not rewarded for above-average profit on the account, but for quality of account team performance and client satisfaction.
   D. Involve the agency in your business:
      1. Provide them with more information than they need—marketing plans, sales analyses, salesmen's reports, lab reports—about your specific business.
      2. Invite them to visit the factory, sales meetings, management conferences, trade shows; the more they know about your business in general, the better they can help you.
      3. Take a writer and media buyer to lunch; get to know *their* business.
   E. Be sure the agency is adequately compensated for the work you expect of them.

F. Pay agency invoices on time so that agency does not have to use its own funds to cover media invoices.

G. Avoid misunderstandings by having written summaries of the basis for compensation, explicit billing procedures, and normal lead times for production that, if adhered to, will avoid overtime charges.

H. Insist the agency provide conference reports on all client contacts, delivered to your office within two days.

I. When there is a problem, bring it up immediately. If not resolved to your satisfaction, go higher up in agency management chain. Annually, prepare a written evaluation of the agency; document the good, the bad, and the ugly.

J. Write letter or send an e-mail to agency management when a member of account team provides exceptional contribution.

II. Agency compensation

A. Compensation is based on many factors:

1. Number of ads prepared.

2. Number of services from agency.

3. Number of client approval levels.

4. Number of times plans and budgets changed during year.

5. Amount of information supplied to agency.

6. Detail involved in media purchases.

B. Service expectations:

1. Rule of thumb: Between 25% and 33% of agency income on an account will go to direct salaries to those working on that account.

2. *Example:* If there's $1 million in billing and agency income is $150,000 (15%), then the agency would put between $38,000 and $50,000 in salaries against account.

C. Forms of compensation
   1. Commission
      a. Usually 15% of gross on media and production materials purchased. For the client, the advantage is that the amount varies with budget and is easy to compute; disadvantage is that it's not related to amount or quality of service.
      b. For the agency, the advantage is that it shares in success as the budget grows; disadvantage is if the budget is cut back at end of year when all the work is done, budget may be too small to generate income to cover services demanded.
   2. Retainer
      a. Monthly fee that may amount to more or less than 15% commission, but must be paid regardless of budget fluctuations.
      b. For the client, the advantage is that it's related to amount of service rendered; the disadvantage, that it must be paid even if budget is severely reduced.
      c. For the agency, the advantage is an even cash flow with an assured certain income; disadvantage is they do not share benefits of increased sales and advertising budget.
   3. Flat fee
      a. A stated or negotiated fee for a given project or type of work. Usually in addition to commission or retainer.
      b. Can be used for art direction, mechanical preparation, creative work on collateral promotion material, supervision of research projects, concept work for new products, etc.

    c. For the client, the advantage is compensation related to service; disadvantage is determining appropriate fee.

    d. For agency, advantage is providing income for extra services, supplemental payments can be requested if original negotiated fee is inadequate; disadvantage is that client may think the agency is charging too much.

4. Cost plus

    a. Agency income is based on actual costs plus guaranteed profit such as 10%, billed monthly.

    b. For the client, advantage is related to service provided; disadvantage is that it may result in more service than is needed.

    c. For the agency, the advantage is the assurance it can meet client requirements and still make profit; disadvantage is it is limited to average profit, and accounting is complicated.

5. Bonus

    a. Additional compensation to agency for meeting stated goal or goals.

    b. Goals may be share of market, sales, and/or awareness and preference—or anything else the client and the agency have agreed on.

6. Combinations

    a. Any combination of above methods may be appropriate for a given client. Some examples follow.

    b. Monthly retainer plus 5% commission.

    c. For industrial accounts, 15% commission plus flat fee for creative work on each ad.

    d. Monthly retainer for account service, flat fee for creative work, media purchased in-house.

III. Agency evaluations
   A. Informal evaluation
      1. Several times a year you should evaluate the agency and take steps to fix problems before they become unmanageable
      2. Yardsticks:
         a. Are our ads better than our competitors?
         b. Are projects moving ahead of schedule?
         c. Does account team understand our business?
         d. Is billing timely, accurate, and within estimate?
   B. Formal evaluation
      1. Objective: improve advertising.
      2. Danger: discourage or alienate agency personnel.
      3. Essential: perspective on relative importance of factors being rated; for example, creative quality is more important than timely conference reports.
      4. Develop checklist of factors of performance related to your needs. If rating scale used, also provide for statements why high or low ratings were given, as well as providing an overall evaluation of strengths and weaknesses of the agency.
      5. Get input from and review evaluation with your management concerned with agency performance.
      6. Review written evaluation personally with head of agency and account representatives. Request written response from agency in two weeks.
IV. Letter of agreement
   A. Services to be performed by agency.
   B. Compensation based on:
      1. Media space.
      2. Media production.
      3. Creative fees.
      4. Sales promotion.

     5. Research.

     6. Printing.

     7. Agency travel.

     8. Other compensation.

     9. Items billable without compensation.

C. Agency legal liability/indemnity for ad content and product performance.

D. Right to review pertinent agency records.

E. Financial working procedures.

     1. Terms of payment of invoices.

     2. Billing of production and sales promotion on completion or monthly as accrued.

     3. Cash discount.

     4. Estimates for expenditures over $200 with revisions if they are exceeded by 10%.

     5. Client approval procedures.

     6. When competitive bids are required.

     7. Media invoices submitted no more than 30 days prior to being due to media; client allowed 10 days to pay agency.

     8. Non-media invoices supported with copies of invoices from outside suppliers.

F. Termination.

     1. Must give 90-day notice.

     2. Compensation provided during 90 days.

     3. All materials and information to be returned.

V. Terminating the agency

A. Give three months to perform to your satisfaction.

B. If no improvement, give notice of termination with compensation to continue for 90 days or as stated in letter of agreement.

C. Work out dates when termination will be announced to agency personnel, client personnel, and to the press.

VI. Selecting a new agency
   A. Determine your criteria for a new agency.
      1. Services required.
      2. Size of agency relative to your budget.
      3. Agency experience in your business.
      4. Local versus out of town.
      5. Preferred amount and method of compensation.
   B. Select ten or twelve contenders.
      1. Agencies doing ads you admire.
      2. Suggestions from other ad managers.
      3. Yellow pages.
      4. Red Book (standard directory of agencies).
      5. Ad Club, BPAA.
      6. AD AGE billing issue.
      7. Media representatives.
      8. Consultant.
   C. Contact contenders.
      1. Letter or e-mail to agency head
         a. Ask if interested and if any conflicts.
         b. Tell them who you are; send products, budget, annual reports.
         c. If they are interested, ask to visit office for a one-hour tour and conversation.
         d. If they aren't interested, ask them to recommend other agencies.
      2. Visit agency office to check for:
         a. Chemistry/personalities.
         b. Number of employees.
         c. Atmosphere.
         d. List of current clients.
         e. Permission to contact certain clients.
      3. Cut down your prospects to between three and five and ask them for formal presentations.

D. Handling inquiries
  1. Have ready response to the press and to agencies not on contender list.
  2. For press, "no comment" or prepared statement with optional facts, such as:
     a. List of contending agencies.
     b. Why the former agency was terminated.
     c. Whether additional agencies will be considered.
     d. Amount of advertising budget.
     e. When decision on new agency will be made.
  3. Set up a system to handle agencies who call.
     a. Send information on company.
     b. Send questionnaire on their list of clients, billings, number of employees, sample of print ads, why they might do a good job for you.
E. Formal presentation
  1. Length: three hours. Portion of meeting to cover set questions, content of the remainder of time should be left to the agency. Provide written guidelines. Allow three weeks preparation.
  2. Set questions to be covered:
     a. Agency history.
     b. List of clients.
     c. Selection of ads done by creative people still at agency.
     d. Background of key people.
     e. How they plan to learn your business.
     f. How they typically develop a campaign.
     g. How they typically develop a media plan.
     h. How they charge for services.
     i. Special services you may require.

    3. Specify in advance whether or not you will look at speculative creative work and if the agencies will be compensated for same.

    4. Specify that any ideas advanced to you may be used by you with no, or specified, compensation to the agency.

F. Implementing the decision.

    1. Make decision within 24 hours.

    2. Make sure compensation arrangements are clear.

    3. If the agency is small, check its credit rating.

    4. Call losers personally and follow with thank-you letter.

    5. Send a case of champagne to agency on the same day that you notify them of their appointment.

    6. Work out letter of agreement.

Index